Ordinary Movings

Joyce

Karen Moores-Cleary

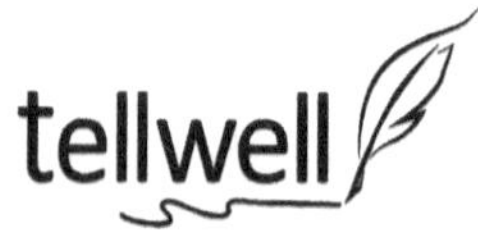

Tellwell Talent
www.tellwell.ca

ISBN
978-0-2288-6174-4 (Paperback)
978-0-2288-6175-1 (eBook)

Acknowledgements

The list is long, but in particular, I would like to thank Robert Cleary for his understanding, Jason Hewer and Scott Hewer for their enthusiasm, Glen Moores for his insight, Pat Kostal for her valuable feedback, Fred and Jo Hughes for their kindness, Anjelee French for her presence, Linda Rule for her inspiration, Heather Patterson for her understanding, and all my dear lifelong friends in Canada and wonderful new ones in Europe. An enormous expression of gratitude goes to Tellwell as well, for the wonderful guidance throughout this writing process. You are all part of this story. While this book is based on a true story, characters and situations have been fictionalised. It has been researched for historical accuracy but any errors are strictly my own.

...For my mother,
and every child growing up away from home...

$\mathcal{A}$ true story of how in 1930's Canada, a mother's financial struggles led to a decision to send her twelve-year-old daughter two thousand miles from home. An only daughter with four brothers, Joyce leaves her Toronto home to live with her maiden aunt in western Canada for two years. The solitary train journey to begin life away from her family, while piqued with colourful characters, leads to ongoing alienation. On arrival in the west, Joyce's kindly aunt provides a stable, nurturing home, but the timid outsider struggles to make new friends. She then meets a young Native boy, who, in the wisdom of the authorities of the day, was taken from his home on the reserve to be fostered in the city. The bond she forms with him initially helps her to adjust, until his own problems overtake, and they too are separated.

Joyce focuses on her schoolwork. She practises mental arithmetic and French conjugations in her head on her way home from school. She does well academically, but never really recovers from her feelings of rejection.

Returning eventually to her home in Toronto, Joyce has trouble resettling. Homecoming is not quite what she imagines. The experience of growing up alone is echoed by successive generations, as reflected latterly in the voice of Joyce's daughter Alana.

A story of families torn apart for economic survival. The aftermath of early twentieth century divorces, the role played by the government of the day, pioneering single mothers, and their legacies are prominent themes. The trauma suffered by children who are separated from their families, can brew devastating problems for decades to come.

Joyce's story, while full of heartache, is brightened with lighter moments of humour and tenderness. While based on true events, some names have been changed and some characters fictionalised.

Toronto, 1938

How could corduroy be cold? Tiny bumps had sprouted on her legs, meeting the ridged brown fabric on the train seat under her long skirt. She noticed tiny hairs were standing up away from her white ankles. They must be half an inch long. As she spotted them, her nose wrinkled. They looked foreign to her. She should have worn two pairs of woollen socks under her skirt.

She pulled her worn hat down over her blonde head, wrapped her scarf more tightly around her, and shivered into her not-quite-warm-enough coat.

On the platform in the distance, she could still see her mother in her navy suit and tilted hat, waving with one hand and clutching Billy's tiny fist with the other. Lifting her arm to wave back, Joyce's stomach churned. She felt sick; "nauseous"

Mother called it. She turned her head away from her family and faced the direction the train would be going. "Sit facing forward," her mother had commanded. "If you look back the way you've come, you'll get dizzy, queasy." Joyce wasn't sure if her stomach had listened.

Whistling its shrill last call, the train's pistons hissed, and people waved from the platform. The carriage lurched. It was about to move! Unable to stop herself, Joyce turned back for one last glimpse of her family. She waved limply at Mother and then at Billy, his angelic face gradually blurring, then fading away in the distance, as the train spat and lurched away from them.

When the young traveller could no longer make out their shapes on the platform, she shuddered and tugged down her skirt. Her hand reached down beside her, to find her small suitcase in the aisle. She clutched it, keeping it close. It contained a few blouses and skirts, another cardigan, her Sunday dress, and socks and undergarments of course. There was also a letter from her mother, a lucky stone Andrew had given her, along with a book, and a tiny toy bear from Billy. With a little nod, the toddler had placed it in Joyce's hand before they said goodbye. Also inside the luggage was her music medal, a small, sharp-edged object of brass awarded with surprise when she passed her Grade 5 conservatory exam. The examiner had declared, "It's not that you've got talent so much, as the fact that you worked hard."

Outside her window, the hooded entrances stretched toward the grandness of Union Station, with its busyness of travellers and workers. Flanking the station was the grey city, which formed a hard square outline, making Joyce think of Billy's building blocks.

She hadn't had time to count the passenger cars, but before boarding, had noticed there were seven empty coal cargo cars trailing behind, with the bright red caboose signalling the end of the train.

Her family didn't own a motor car. But during those rare times, when the family had accepted a ride in a car from one of the family members, they occasionally found themselves held up behind railway barriers as a train crossed their path. She remembered her mother suddenly taking her by surprise - chanting out the names of the different carriages. "Engine, passenger car, passenger, passenger car, passenger car, diner car, cargo car, cargo car, errr ... coal car, coal car, uh ... coal car ... errr, uh ... cargo car ... caaaaa-boose!" Her confident calls were interrupted by laughter from the others when she hesitated to name a carriage.

Joyce wondered whether her mother might have lingered with Billy today to see if they could see another train and play the game again. Unlikely. Her mother didn't have much time for games these days ... if ever.

Returning to the inside of the chilly carriage with her thoughts, the words of her eldest brother, Andrew, came to mind. "If cold could make a sound," he used to say, "it could almost make its own noises, like a harsh squeal when your skin meets the cold porcelain in the bath before the water goes in ... or crunching through the crust of ice covered snow." He used to say the cold sounded before it was felt. "It warns you that way, a few seconds ahead." Now, it surely was the shrill whistle and creak of the train as it inched away from the station, and away from her life. And Andrew ... Andrew was "university material," her dad used to say, adding, "but ..." Often repeated, the sentence was never finished.

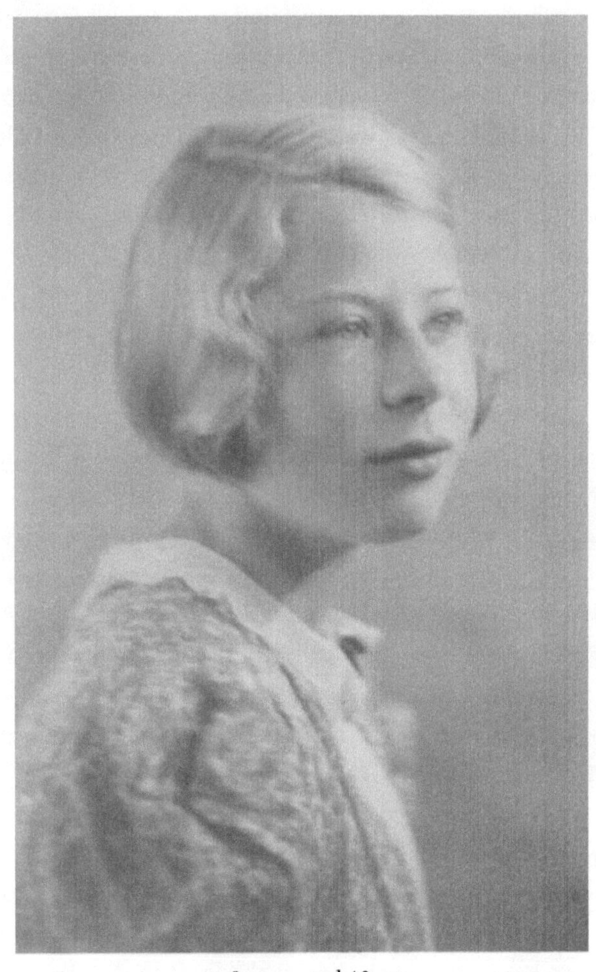

Joyce, aged 12

Material

"Material? How could a person be that?" Joyce thought about the corduroy under her, the material the train seat was made from. And the cotton in her blouses, the wool in her cardigans. That was material. They had used different types of material in sewing class. Thinking about the word had made her shudder. Probably because at the very same time as she heard the word, she had felt Miss Watson pressing bony fingers into her shoulders. "Bunching, bunching! The material is bunching, don't you see? You need to take your stitching out and start again.... Do it properly," her teacher had said, accusingly. Joyce had never been very good at domestic science.

She was better at boys' subjects really. Or at least some of them. Funny to think about it. She didn't really like the sewing and cooking of domestic science at all, she much preferred history, and geography. History because it involved stories of the adventures of explorers, their grand sailing vessels and discovery of new lands, and geography as it was about everything about those lands—mountains and lakes, and plant life, why things grew in some places and not others, and how people lived. Those "boy" things were really interesting to Joyce.

Now her own geography was changing. She was on an adventure. She would be exploring.... Andrew had said as much. But ... she started to think of her other school subjects.

Science was also interesting. She thought of the wet rag her teacher had scrunched up at the front of the classroom and placed beside a flattened out one to show which one dried more quickly. That was evaporation. They had also measured a cup of water, poured it into a pot and watched it boil. After it was boiling for five minutes, they let it cool and measured the liquid again. It was less than a cup. Some of the water had evaporated. There was a lot more she would like to know about these things.

Mathematics—another boys' thing really. "Let's see … nine times tables. Nine times two is 18, nine times three is 27, nine times four is 36…"

She even did fairly well at mathematics. But then, her marks had gone down a fair bit recently.

Leaning her cheek against the window, Joyce watched dirtying ripples of snow caking the curbs. Steep banks lining the railway line were capped in a grimy film of slush, like grey icing left untouched, discoloured after a white layer cake was long gone. Along with the steel city buildings, it was all ebbing away.

Her solitary journey was only just beginning. And turning her attention inside the train didn't do much to assuage her uneasiness. Suddenly, a strange feeling crept over her shoulders. Her icy cheek came unglued from the window; she straightened up fast in her seat and turned around to see white eyes peering out at her near the top of a dark round face.

Men Missing

"Where you headed, little lady? Next stop will be Richmond Hill."

It wasn't the man her mother had instructed from the platform, saying, "Make sure she gets off in Edmonton, please?" Joyce had never seen this man before, what did Mother call him again, the conductor"?

Joyce in fact had never seen a black man before, but mother had read from a large fairy tale book called *Aesop's Fables* when she was little. It featured stories and pictures of Africa, and Joyce adored the stories. But she never expected to be face to face with … what did Mother say they were called? "Negroes' '! "They are no different from us, Joyce," her mother had hastened to add. "Only the colour of our skin is different."

"I-I'm going to Edmonton, to my aunt's house," she stammered, showing her ticket. The fine hairs on her wrists stood to attention, matching the ones on her legs.

"Oh, my, that's a long way! I thought because you're on your own, maybe you were just on a short trip. Well … don't worry. We'll all take good care of you. Hey, you cold? I can bring you a blanket if you'd like. Enjoy the countryside. Travelling by train is wonderful," he declared, clipping her ticket with a snap. Large white teeth gleamed from his mouth, as he nodded to her and quickly disappeared along the aisle.

Strangely, she now wished he had stayed a little longer. And she wasn't quick enough to say yes to the blanket before he disappeared!

Joyce thought now how rarely she saw men at all these days. Her best friend Marg's father was a salesman and often away from home. In fact, he rarely even saw Marg, let alone Joyce overlapping with him the few times he was at home. But at least Marg's father still lived with them. Joyce couldn't remember the last time she'd seen her father. Was it last year sometime …?

It seemed hard to believe that she wouldn't be seeing Marg each day, skipping together on their way to and from school, and playing together at one another's houses. It was even harder to think that it would be at least two years until she saw her best friend or her brothers again. The rhythmical chugga-um chugging and hissing of the train were the backdrop for her moony thoughts.

Sighing heavily, Joyce dreaded the thought of being away from her friend for so long; she felt she could talk to Marg about so many things. Not everything, maybe, but a lot of things. And her brother Andrew too. She always felt quite protected when he was around. Robert and David, well she probably wouldn't miss them too much, she had to admit. But Andrew ... and ahhh, Billy ... sweet Billy!

Brothers

She thought then of her four brothers and how different they were. Not from her of course; they were not like her at all. Obviously. She was female and they were male. But the four of them—two older, two younger—were nothing like one another. Nothing at all.

As the eldest, Andrew's job was clearing up after meals every night, washing the dishes, while the others took turns drying. At least these were her mother's new rules since their father had gone away. Joyce thought how much things had changed since then. Andrew used to sometimes find time to sit down with her for a game of some sort after dinner or help her with her homework. Occasionally he would even listen to her practise on the piano. But since her father left, it had all changed. Now, each evening when chores were done, he always disappeared to his room for homework and studying. Andrew always seemed to have so much more homework than

Robert. In fact, he seemed to have more homework than the rest of them put together!

Robert had explained to Joyce that "being university material" had meant that their eldest brother Andrew was really clever. "But don't tell him that, Jocie," Robert added quickly. "He'll get a swelled head." Then he gave her shoulder a quick jostle, nearly sending her books slipping out of her arms before whisking away.

He always disappeared like that before she could tell him not to call her Jocie, the babyish name her youngest brother Billy always called her. He knew it annoyed her; it was his way of taking the upper hand. Then he would be out the door as quick as flash. Robert would often say he had a football match after school and speed off.

Whereas Andrew was dark-haired, not too tall, and wore glasses, Robert already towered above his older brother. The second eldest often appeared at the dinner table with his wavy blond hair tousled. Once or twice, Joyce asked him if she could go with him, but he said the game was too rough for girls. It seemed to Joyce that there was a football activity almost every day. If not, Robert would go to the park with his friends so he could "throw a ball around." He never seemed to miss a game or a practice, and Joyce never asked to go again. She did wonder sometimes why Robert was allowed to be out so much; her mother didn't seem to mind. Her mother had mentioned something about Robert going to university as well, because he could get a scholarship, which was something to do with being good at playing football. But this didn't really make any sense to Joyce. Wasn't university just like a school for older boys who were really, really smart? Still, she somehow felt she shouldn't ask Robert too much about it. Better to get Andrew to explain this to her.

Joyce's nickname, Jocie, had been pronounced that way by Billy when he hadn't been quite two, and to an extent, it had been adopted by the rest of the family. But Joyce always felt strongly that it was only Billy who was allowed to use it. She never minded when he said it, but somehow when the others did, it made her seethe. They knew full well she was too grown up for the babyish name. Billy didn't know any better, so that was different. Her little brother loved to scramble onto her lap for a story, his chubby, soft wrists brushing against her skin. His blue eyes would fix on her as she read him stories or sang him a lullaby. She would stroke his creamy arms until he wrestled them away from her and started to squirm to get down. Always too early for Joyce's liking, he would quickly wriggle off her lap in search of his toy cars. Or, too soon, he would be collected by Mother with the order of "bedtime," resisting his mother's grasp while rubbing his eyes.

Today on the platform, that pudgy hand had twisted to and fro, as he tried to copy the motions of their mother as she waved Joyce off. Billy was two and a half now and would change so much by the next time she saw him. Would he even remember her? Joyce shuddered and sighed into the October air.

Then there was David, two years younger than her. A bespectacled 10-year-old, her brother always seemed quicker at everything than Joyce was. Certainly, at school. Although she had been a fairly good B student, David always surpassed her at report card time. She didn't care for David all that much if she was honest. Not because he did better at school.

It was mainly because her mother kept repeating that because he was younger than her, she should be looking after him, and "setting an example." The trouble was he never played by the rules.

One day, quite a long time ago as Joyce remembered it—in fact it still bothered her now—an orange had appeared in the house. The fruit was a rare treat. "I'll cut and you choose," he had said, following his mother's suggestion for sharing the juicy temptation. David sliced a small wedge off the orange, grabbed the big piece and ran off. Startled, she wailed out a protest, but her mother, who was busy working upstairs, admonished her, telling her not to be childish.

David had desperately wanted to go on this journey across Canada, but it was never to be. People in their household did not often get the things they really wanted. Not long after her Dad had moved away, a letter to Joyce's mother had arrived from Edmonton from Aunt Lorna, suggesting that one of the five children come to live with her in the west for a couple of years.

Andrew had tried to explain the idea to Joyce. He said her maiden aunt was hoping to help relieve some of the financial burden on the now fatherless family. With four boys and only one girl, her aunt had expected her mother to write back with news that she had agreed to send one of the boys. Obviously, Billy was too young to leave his mother, and as her elder brothers were teenagers, they could potentially help their mother by earning some extra money after school. Instead, it was decided that Joyce would be packed off to the west.

The story repeated itself in her head, as southern Ontario sped past, the agricultural land giving way to rolling forests and lakes. It should have been David on this train. Instead, she sat now, shivering in the unheated carriage, wondering what life lay ahead of her in the Rockies, and even over the next few days, on long the train ride to get there.

Robert had seemed a bit upset too, she thought. "But why does she get to go, Mother? She's going to get to see the Rockies and everything while we have to stay home. She's younger than me. How come she gets to go before I do?!"

"You can go, you go, David and Robert," Joyce harumphed through her thoughts. "I'll stay home with Andrew and Billy. I'll stay home, you can go," she willed silently and hopelessly. It would have made everyone—or almost everyone—so much happier! But as it was, no one was really happy. Although, as she thought more about it, she felt sure that neither David nor Robert seemed to mind their sister going away for two years!

Dirty Thirties

"Chucka-chucka-uum-mumm, chucka-uum-mumm," the train sputtered.

As she sat alone on the double seat in a deserted carriage, Joyce wondered if anyone else would get on the train at the next stop, and if the passenger car would warm up just a little. Then Joyce remembered that Mother had said she wouldn't be surprised if the late autumn mid-week train were quite empty because the adults would all be working and children would be in school. There certainly were no other passengers around her, so far, and she sighed heavily as she looked at the dull brown-and-grey carriage and contemplated two days and two nights alone on the icy train.

Her memories then drifted back to something Andrew had said to her in the summertime. Looking up from his text book, Andrew had said, "We're now in the 'Dirty Thirties,' you know, Joyce." It was declared, as though it was an answer to all her questions.

"Dirty? Why dirty?" Joyce asked.

"It means we're in a depression, Joyce," Andrew explained gently. "After the war, people are still getting back on their feet. There's no work, food is scarce, you know. The rationing we have at the moment—only so much coal for heating, not much butter, eggs for each family. Things are hard now. There's not much money around."

Travelling Menu

Joyce decided to finally open her clenched fist to look at the letter her mother had handed to her as she said goodbye.

> *Dear Joyce,*
>
> *You have enough money to last you the three days until you get to Aunt Lou's, so do not squander it.*

Joyce pondered on her mother's shortening of her Aunt Lorna's name. If she had shortened her Aunt Ida's name, it would just be "I." She coughed out a tiny laugh.

> *The sandwiches I gave you should be enough until tomorrow, if you eat one at lunch time and one in the evening. Do not spend anything until*

tomorrow and do not buy any snacks for between meals. When I met you after your car trip to Aunt Ida's, I was shocked to find the back seat covered in peanut shells. I have brought you up with better manners than that, and this is only something someone with bad breeding would do! So please remember that and this time think of what I have taught you.

Then tomorrow, you can eat the apple I gave you for breakfast and if it's not too much, you should be able to afford a bowl of soup and some bread for your lunch. Please remember to dip the spoon away from you into the soup and take it from the far edge of the bowl. The soup will help to warm you up because if you think it's cold here, you wait until you get to the Rockies. There will be snow on the mountain tops almost all year round out there. You will probably sleep in the afternoons on the train anyway, so you don't need so much to eat. In the evenings, there will probably be a stew or something for dinner in the dining car. Remember, you're a very lucky girl to be going on this adventure, my Dear."

Joyce sighed. The idea of food didn't tempt her in the slightest at the moment.

The letter also told her to find a seat near the toilet so that if "nature called" she would cause the least possible disturbance to the other passengers.

> *They might be sleeping, reading or engaged*
> *in conversation, so you stay near the restrooms,*
> *Dear, and keep yourself to yourself.*

But the conductor had told her where she must sit; she was given no choice. Then she remembered the conductor telling her about the train stopping at Barrie. She knew enough not to go to the toilet during stops. The train was speeding along now; they must have stopped at Barrie while she was reading the letter, and she hadn't noticed. The train seemed to be about to stop again, judging from the hissing sounds it was making.

Anyway, "what other passengers?" she wondered. Her mother had contradicted herself, because at first, she said the train would likely be fairly clear of passengers. Then she said not to disturb them! In fact, despite having stopped at least twice now, no new travellers had joined the carriage.

The letter droned on.

> *The sandwiches have my currant jam in them*
> *so they won't go bad. They will last overnight.*
> *David has even given you an orange, very kindly*
> (this part made Joyce groan), *so keep that for*
> *tomorrow or even the next day. Aunt Lorna has*
> *been so kind to us and has generously even sent a*
> *little money for the train, but you have to make*
> *that last. Don't forget, no peanuts! And remember*
> *what I told you. Go to bed early, make sure you*
> *take a top berth, do not sleep on a bottom one and*
> *make sure to close the curtains around the berth. I*
> *don't want anyone peeking in at you!*

> *Have a good trip and don't forget to give*
> *Aunt Lou the envelope in your suitcase. Write to*
> *me as soon as you get there, and I will write back*
> *when I have the time.*
>
> *Love, Mother.*

Historic Voyages

The train trailed through the Midlands. In the textbooks back home were accounts of many renowned explorers venturing along the Great Lakes and surrounding wilderness. The voyageurs, laden with furs and trading goods, forged through the St. Lawrence Seaway, battling the elements often with meagre supplies or reinforcements. Were these difficult journeys across the ocean, penetrating foreign frontiers made without trepidation? As they tread across enormous distances from their homeland, was there no hint of worry or doubt seeded into their personal effects?

In one such account in the early 1600s, Jean de Brébeuf, a Jesuit priest ordained in Rouen, France, volunteered for an international mission to travel to "Nouvelle France" to convert Native Canadian tribes to Christianity and Catholicism. Bound for Quebec and Ontario, he crossed the Atlantic, travelled along the great St. Lawrence Seaway, north of Lake Erie and on to the Midland area.

Tribal customs of the day involved worshipping animals and the natural elements and Brébeuf strove to "enlighten" these Indigenous peoples with Catholic religious traditions. However, on arrival, he discovered communication was a challenge and returned to France to study Native language and develop translations suitable for the catechism.

He then brought these new texts to "Nouvelle France" in what would embolden history texts in later years. The mission of conversion proved a struggle, but Brébeuf declared that he had come not only to live among the Native peoples "but to die with them."

Those, among other immortalised quotations, were, some conclude, divine premonitions. In Canada in the 1600s, dispelling tribal beliefs and customs were not the only forces opposing the missionary. During a raid on the Hurons by the Iroquois, Brébeuf, along with the Native community, was tortured mercilessly. The invading tribe then famously ate his heart and drank his blood. Later captured in stained glass "en couleurs vivantes" in his home church in France, Brébeuf is depicted cradling his heart.

The French priest was ultimately canonised, and as one of the Canadian martyrs, became the Patron Saint of Canada. His grave lies enshrined in St. Ignace, Ontario near Ste. Marie. In France, the ruins of his family manor were rebuilt in the 1990s as a chapel and shrine in Sainte-Suzanne-sur-Vire in Normandy, France.

Journeys within Journeys

As she finished the letter, a fresh shudder crept across her twelve-year-old shoulders. Joyce began to worry how she could slip past the train workers to the toilet and the sleeping car when it was time to go to bed. She didn't want to draw attention to herself.

Craning her neck along the length of the carriage, she tried to spy the sleeping cars farther along the train. The cold was bad enough, but the prospect of spending the night on the train by herself filled her with dread. The creeping thoughts paired up with the chilly temperature to send trembles through her.

"Be brave," the brotherly sounds of wisdom echoed heavily in her ears. They were Andrew's words of comfort as last evening, he held her tightly for their long goodbye. "You're strong, Joyce, and very smart, so don't worry, you'll be all right. Just think ... you get to be away from your brothers for two years! That should cheer you up! You'll probably love it there and forget all about us!" As Andrew said his goodbyes and tried to tease her, she choked down a little sob, knowing she had better not be caught crying.

She folded the letter over and placed it back in her shoulder bag with another shudder. Then, quickly gathering herself, she bolted off her seat, sweeping her hand across the cold ribs of corduroy. Quickly jumping up as the train slowed down, she chose to move in the direction the train was going, hoping she would find the toilets at that end. Keeping her eyes straight ahead, she strode forward along the narrow aisle. Once she was vertical rather than seated, the train seemed to move sideways as much as it was travelling forward. Bracing herself on the arms of the seats, she walked her hands as well as her feet along the length of the carriage.

As she looked down, she could see her feet stepping onto the metal plates which joined up the next carriage. Joyce could see train tracks racing beneath her. Swiftly, she lunged into the next carriage, where she was rocked sideways across the car and into a brown sleeve. Hands came out of a suit jacket to steady her. Another passenger! Then, feeling older eyes on her, she willed herself to look ahead and avoid meeting his gaze.

"Whoa little lady." There was a sour scent of something, and a large hand rose to tip a man's hat while the other hand steadied a buckled briefcase at his feet.

With crimson flooding her cheeks, Joyce dipped in a swift curtsy, blurted out an apology and spun around to return to her seat.

She would wait until the train stopped at the next destination.

Crossing her cold slender legs, she found she didn't need to wait very long. The conductor soon could be heard calling out for passengers who wanted to stop in Barrie.

The train soon ground to a halt, but Joyce could see no passengers either leaving or joining the train. The brown suited man was still there, but fortunately, he had closed his eyes for a nap.

She finally found "the facilities," as her mother called them, and nipped inside as quickly as she could, pee starting to trickle down her leg as the train carelessly jolted her against the toilet wall. The relief came before she spotted a sign in the cubicle: "Do not use when train is in station." Too late. Closing her eyes with a sigh and a prayer, she quickly squatted to release the remaining contents of her bladder, soaped and rinsed her hands in the basin. Then, shaking with nerves and cold, she bustled herself quickly back out of the cubicle to return to her carriage.

The twelve-year-old settled herself back into her seat again. She recognised with a small unavoidable smile that

Muskoka rock had begun to flank the tracks. The sight of them, along with the chugging train, began to lull her. Summery memories began to win over terror, despite herself.

Northern Ontario

It was unmistakable! The twelve-year-old had thought relatively little about the geography of her journey really; just that she knew it was a long one! She should have asked Andrew to tell her more about it. But, as the Muskoka landscape thrust itself into her view, it was as though it had been chasing her to bid farewell and had finally caught up with her. Rugged stones in pinks and greys, endless blue lakes. Muskoka was her summer comfort blanket, and here it was following her into her autumn journey!

Joyce's Aunt Ida, her mother's eldest sister, was the widow of a wealthy inventor. Family history had it that he had devised a clever pulley system that made a small fortune, and he and his family lived lavishly for generations from the royalties. After his death, Ida was, as Joyce's mother had explained, "the matriarch, the real head of the family." She owned an island in Muskoka, at Foot's Bay, where Joyce and her brothers had often been invited to stay for two-week summer holidays. Joyce's cousins, Chas and Margaret, much older than her, would pick them up in their cars, and take them three hours north to Lake Joseph, where they were collected by rowboat from the marina to take them in twos across to the island. There, they spent long days, swimming off the rocks, playing endless games of badminton and backgammon, and enjoying delicious meals served by a stout maid. Joyce and her brothers had wished they could linger there all summer, but Aunt Ida had a schedule with plenty of other guests coming, so they savoured every minute of what was for them, a luxury holiday.

Joyce recalled now how the old lady in her starchy suit and neat silver bun came to visit them in Toronto regularly. Or, rather, to inspect, as her mother had said. The family of five were lined up outside the house while Aunt Ida marched past them, giving each individual either an reluctant nod or a disapproving scowl. Occasionally, she straightened a collar or two. "She's 23 years older than I am you see," her mother had explained. "Kind of like a second mother. So we need to be respectful for her!" In later years, it became clear that pleasing Ida was necessary to assist the family budget.

Although her mother's letter hadn't done much to trigger Joyce's appetite, she decided to open her supplies anyway and began eating the jam sandwich. The black currants were slightly tart. As she ate, she wondered what kind of life was waiting for her in the west.

Was Aunt Lou anything like Aunt Ida? Were they alike? Joyce shivered at the thought. After all, they were the closest in age of all her mother's family. But then Aunt Ida had children of course, whereas Aunt Lou didn't. She liked Aunt Ida; she was quite kind to them, but her visits were so formal and seemed to make her mother even crosser and stricter with them than usual.

Joyce began to think that her mother was really lucky to have so many sisters. How many was it? Ida, Lorna, Sadie, Maude (who sadly died), Margaret (who also sadly died) and Elsie ... that was ... four sisters still alive! Yet Joyce had none. Instead, she had four brothers! Still, as the train lurched along ... she began to feel a little badly about her unkind thoughts toward Robert and David. She couldn't imagine life without any of her brothers really.

New Terrain

Joyce fixed her fresh eyes out the window, watching as the scenery changed. Now the landscape was offering up steep cliffs and waterfalls, while the trees had changed from oak, elm and apple to silver birch, spruce, pine and hemlock. Everything looked very different to what she had left behind in Toronto.

Fields were steadily becoming a seamless quilt of white. She couldn't remember ever having seen snow this early before! As the carriages veered north and slightly west, dark evergreens towered above them, dwarfing their neighbouring birch trees. Lazy lakes, and rivers foaming over rocks were flashing by Joyce's window view. Sporadically, clusters of small towns crested the hillsides. For a time, the beauty of the scenery stole Joyce's attention, and she forgot herself for a while.

Then, unexpectedly, glints of sunlight glanced off the snow, making Joyce avert her gaze for a moment. Uninvited, her melancholy returned, descending its heaviness upon her again. Buildings dotted rather than crowded her view—a lonely greeting for Joyce's wet eyes. Pursing her lips, she turned to the empty seats inside the carriage. Their brownness, their uniform stiffness made her think of soldiers going off to war.

With the steady numbing rhythm of the train reflecting her mood, her eyelids were becoming heavy and gently, she dropped off to sleep, missing the signs for Sault Ste.

Marie which sprouted along the tracks. The "midway point" in Ontario, the station used some of the last bricks of the province, a stout and sturdy landmark, but Joyce dosed through.

Her soft blonde hair was matted slightly around her ears when she awoke a little while later. Giving her eyes a little rub, she noticed the houses were now made of clapboard rather than brick. Sometimes battered with strips missing, they were more fragile looking than the permanent homes she was used to in the south. Signs began to sprout for Iroquois Falls and Sioux Lookout. Even the language seemed to be changing.

She had been fascinated when Andrew had explained that Native peoples inhabited many communities along the north shore of Lake Superior. "You will see signs for places where the various tribes are living, such as Algonquin, Huron, Iroquois."

Wide eyed at his description, but not wanting to appear completely ignorant, she asked him what sort of houses they lived in. Smiling the older brother smile, Andrew simply said, "That you will have to see for yourself, so don't forget to write and tell me!"

As the train trundled along the north shore of Lake Superior, through the rugged terrain, strange, small communities began to pop up. Joyce noticed a few dwellings clumped together rather haphazardly, and in the front yards, sat the occasional cluster of men in bright woollen sweaters amongst discarded tools, leather straps, and furnishings.

Fellow Passengers

Joyce realised she needed the toilet again—had she not just been a short time ago?—just when she felt a little more at ease with her journey, which somehow seemed friendlier as the scenery changed. Groaning inwardly, she got up to begin another journey inside the train. At least this time she knew where the toilet was.

As she edged along to her destination, a woman in a white silk blouse, pearl necklace and dirndl skirt slipped out of the small door marked WC and into the carriage. Patent leather high heels clipped toward Joyce, who kept her eyes lowered, imagining a penetrating gaze of disdain on her head. She dug her top teeth into her lower lip, pursed her lips together, and filled her cheeks with air. Then, turning sideways, her eyes slid over full bosoms inside the silk blouse. Joyce realised this fellow passenger was smiling a little at her. She wasn't gathering herself to criticize. The woman slipped past the brown suited man Joyce had seen before and sunk into the window seat beside him.

There WERE other people on this train! Joyce wasn't really sure which she preferred—deserted cars or inhabited ones.

Breathing again, the twelve-year-old edged into the link between carriages. She felt her heart thump with the roar of the train in that split-second space where there seemed to be just land under her. "Quick, quick, quick, quick," the train seems to chug at her, "get into the next carriage."

Lining the aisle, were more brown and black suits. "Businessmen," Mother would have called them. One or two she could only see when she was parallel with them. Their faces and bodies were hidden by newspapers.

Shouts of "Show, show, show me!" came from a seat toward the end of the carriage.

"Shhh, Billy." For a split second of confusion, Joyce's heart leapt at the sound of her baby brother's name. But too quickly, she realised she was back on the train, and alongside Billy's mother, she saw a chubby boy about seven or eight years old. His mouth gaped open, revealing a pink tongue. His eyes seemed to slant, and he was rocking and swaying against the train motion. He would, as her mother had once explained to her, be mentally retarded.

"We'll be getting off soon, Honey," his mother said, linking her arm through her son's and tilting her head toward him kindly.

Joyce smiled shyly at them but carried on her journey within her journey. Then she suddenly thought, "Where are the sleeping cars?" If only she could find a berth early and go to bed before everyone else, then she would feel safe.

Going to the toilet was put "on hold." She decided to continue through the train.

Arriving in the dining car, she found the carriage empty, except for two uniformed stewards sitting smoking and talking quietly. She then recognised the kindly conductor who had spoken to her back in her own carriage.

"Hello there, Missy, you lost? Your seat is back a few cars in the other direction. You need me to take you back there?"

She wanted to speak as little as possible to anyone. "No, thank you. I'm just looking for my bed, er … my berth."

"Hey, you're early, yet, Honey." He looked at his watch. "Plenty a time yet. In fact, you're too young to give birth!"

He gave her arm a jovial slap. "Hehehehe! I'll let you know when it's your bedtime, don't you worry. You just go on back to your seat. I'll take you to where you sleep when it's time."

"I need a top berth. I must sleep on the top berth."

"Oh, I see … Well, don't you worry 'bout that either, little lass. We all will see to that for you too. You eaten yet? You want a sweet or something?" He stretched out his hand with a tin of boiled sweets.

Droplets of longing formed on her tongue at the sight of the candy, but Joyce felt too shy to accept. Mother. Mother would not approve. "No, no thank you." She dipped into a nervous curtsy. Had her mother taught her that? Swiftly, she then pirouetted around him to continue her search for the sleeping cars.

Flooding the train with banging and thumping was the cargo train next door. As coal was loaded into containers, the noisy process distracted Joyce as she negotiated along the carriages.

New Friends

The next carriage revealed such a different scene it startled, then scared Joyce at first. There was a strong smell of perfume and something like … wet hair. An enormous woman in red-and-black velvet took up two seats on the train, sweat beading her brow and folds in her neck, despite the chill inside the train. Behind her, men in undershirts and suspenders were playing cards and drinking, and another tall skinny man in a cap leaned across the aisle to talk to them. The carriage was crammed with people dressed in all sorts of colourful clothing, and clogging the aisle were bulging suitcases, streaming with kerchiefs looking like ponytails.

"Hey, little lady," a short man with a round belly said, hopping out in front of her. "Where you going?" She tried to squeeze around him, but he grabbed her arm. "No need to be scared a ol' Buster now. Slow up there," he protested, rubbing a mop of ginger hair. "What's ya hurry? You're travellin' faster'n the train there! Whoa, pony!" She tried to escape from his arm, but he had her in a firm grip.

"Hey, Buster, letter go." A tall woman in a tight pink blouse and dark skirt left her seat and pulled Buster away from her. "Leaver alone, now. He's right, tho, lassie, no need a be scared a ol' Buster. He's crazy as a lunatic but gentle as a lamb." Unsure of what a lunatic was, Joyce felt even more nervous.

"Hey, Busty, er Betsy, whatchu talkin' about?"

"Never mind. Keep quiet, Buster! You ok, lassie? What's yer name?" Betsy touched her shoulder.

"Joyce."

"Ok, Joyce, welcome to the circus car!" Betsy put her arm around Joyce and the others cheered. "You travellin' with your Mom and Pa?"

"N-no, I—" Joyce stammered. She didn't want to tell them she was on her own, but it was hard keeping everything to herself all the time. Besides, Buster and Betsy were now blocking the aisle. "I'm taking the train to Alberta to stay with my aunt there."

"Well, you ain't alone now, don't worry. Why don'tcha sit down and have a drink with us?" A man in a checked suit, smelling of smoke was now in the aisle as well. Maps of red veins snaked along his cheeks and nose.

"Don't worry, Len, I'll look after her. You go 'n sit down." Betsy beckoned Joyce to join them and take a seat in the carriage. "We'll be havin' dinner soon. Pull up a pew and join us, Joyce!"

Betsy's smile was kind and she smelled of soft perfume. Joyce hesitated, but the woman's eyes sparkled. Without another thought, Joyce had slid into the seat next to her. Len moved across to the other side of the aisle, looking slightly miffed.

But Betsy shrugged her shoulders at him, and began chatting so warmly to Joyce, that she soon forgot about her solitary quest for the overnight accommodation. Even the urge for the toilet had subsided, as she relaxed into the late afternoon hum in the performers' carriage. Card games were underway, loud voices, plenty of chuckling—there seemed to be some excitement in this car.

Growing ever braver with each passing moment, Joyce explained that she needed the facilities. Betsy then quietly and smoothly took her by the hand to find the water closet, waited outside until she was finished, then guided her back again. Once back in the entertainers' carriage, Betsy introduced her to the others. "Meet Polly, the fat lady. As you can see, Sinbad, the fire eater,—he's new—Raz, the lion tamer, Buster, the musical clown ... on and off stage," she added with a tease. "Len, just along for the ride, and me, I run the show!" Betsy's introductions were interspersed with groans and jeers, but Joyce could feel the closeness within the group.

Then, as the day easily slipped into evening, Joyce felt so much more comfortable, she even accepted their offer to join them for dinner.

"Great," said Betsy, "we've put our order in for six o'clock. You stay put, and your dinner will be served." To her amazement, large steaming dishes arrived on trays carried by smart-suited waiters. Shepherd's pie was then generously heaped on plates for each of them.

"You've heard of room service, Joyce?" quipped Buster. "This is circus service!"

"That's right," Betsy chimed in. "Don't worry, it's all included."

It was a "lapjob," as they called it, balancing their plates on their knees, while digging their forks into the ground beef and potato pie. The meal was the first one she could ever remember eating which was spiced with laughter, teasing and informality.

When a vanilla sponge cake appeared to finish off their dinner, Buster took out a fiddle and started playing the merriest song Joyce had ever heard. A couple of her new companions stood up and started to jig to the tune and Joyce was suddenly transported. It was a completely different journey. Betsy even stood up and grabbed her by the arm, inviting her to clap and toe tap in the aisle along with her. It made nightfall arrive without Joyce noticing. Before she realised it, she was travelling in the dark.

As soon as her awareness returned, the old warning voices accompanied it. Her mother's insistence that she turn in early, and that she must find an upper berth to sleep in was ringing in her ears. Joyce also was to make sure the passenger in the lower berth was a woman, whom her mother said would preferably be asleep before Joyce went to bed. Even Joyce thought this unlikely. And she felt confused as well! If she went to bed at eight o'clock, would an older woman go to bed earlier than that?

Plucking up the courage to explain this to Betsy, the older woman gave her knee a friendly squeeze and insisted Joyce sleep above her that night. The circus worker explained that a few people had left the troop the previous week, and there were a couple of vacancies, so there were several empty beds in their sleeping car.

"Don't worry, Sweetie. I'll look after you," Betsy smiled. "In fact, you look tired already. I'll take you along to bed now. Don't worry, we'll put you in a top berth." Let's go and collect your suitcase, Honey.

Joyce was still a little nervous but followed Betsy as the train rolled and rattled into darkness. A few cars along from the dining car, Betsy boosted her up into an upper berth, gave her a fast hug, pulled the curtain around her, and before the young traveller knew it, she could barely keep her eyes open. Trusting her new friend to return to the lower bunk in a few hours, she was soon enveloped in heavy slumber.

Betsy

Back in the circus car, Betsy was absorbed in a rare reverie of reflection. The young girl would be about the same age as her baby would have been had she lived.

Betsy had only just turned twenty-one when she had joined the circus. She'd had a reasonably happy childhood from a small town in southern Ontario and had made average grades at school. But as the middle child of seven, she sometimes felt crowded out and overlooked. She hadn't wanted the same things as her older siblings—marriage, family and life as a housewife. Her sister Edith, who was closest in age, had spurned marriage for a job, first as a nurse and later training as a nursing educator. But Betsy had always yearned for a life of adventure, excitement and travel.

So when the famous circus barrelled into their small town for the fall fair, she and her girlfriend Sharon saved up their pocket money and arrived at the grounds for opening day. Forgetting time altogether, Betsy and her friend wandered around the whole circus at first, sizing up the midway, with its stuffed animals to be won by throwing darts, catching prizes with a fishing line into a small pool, inhaling the Saturday scents from the popcorn and candy floss stands. She was entranced by the buzz and colour of it all. By four o'clock, Sharon was ready to go home, but Betsy stayed behind, wanting to see the trapeze act. She watched with absorption, the acrobats, the lion tamers, the clowns and jugglers. She was captivated.

However, she still wondered ... if ever she did join the circus, what job would she do? She didn't fit the bill for any of the acts she had seen. She was too slim to be a fat lady, she couldn't juggle to save her life, she was already too old to learn acrobatics, and although reasonably brazen, not enough to tame lions! And yet ... somehow ... she felt she was home from the moment she went through the circus gate.

That was the day she met Len. Older, smelling of cigarette smoke, he wore woodsy jackets, a little too big for him, and a brown cap. He had a sprig of grass in his mouth when he approached her. Although at first sight, he wasn't the man of her dreams, his eyes gleamed with something Betsy had never seen before. Something like ... promise. As though something unexpected was always about to happen. It was a wonderful feeling of ... surprise. Those eyes always hinted of some kind of magic in her future.

He'd offered her a drink, and taking a sip of the sour ale, she winced at the taste. "What is that?" she demanded, leaving her manners at home.

"Just a slosh of beer. Have another taste. You'll like it; t'll relax you. We all drink it here."

He pulled up a bale of hay and suddenly they were sitting chatting together. Len told her he had run away to join the circus as a young lad. His father had been a hard-drinking, hard-hitting type, and since the age of about eleven, the circus had become his home. 'But what is your act?' Betsy was intrigued.

"Setup. That's my act, laughed Len. "Don't have one, ya see. But I have to prepare all the stands for the lions, clean up the hay after the animals have been in the ring, so it's nice and clean for the acrobatic act. Get everyone their grub, their cigarettes for them. They sometimes gripe and snipe at me to get a move on when I'm on me own—I'm often the only one doing their donkey work. But mostly, I'm happy because when it comes down to it ... we're ... we're a ... family! Even if some of the members change every few months."

With circus turnover "changing more often than your underwear" as Len put it, it was easy for Betsy to slide into a role there. She helped the clowns and the fat lady with costumes, did any sewing they wanted, and generally helped to keep the shows running smoothly. And of course, she was close to Len.

He was all right most of the time. He could drink three or four beers in the evening and be just fine. It was for those times when the shadow of his father seemed to creep over him. He'd carried on drinking all evening and would suddenly be consumed with anger and a sharp tongue. It was after one of those binges and apologies that followed when their baby was conceived.

Maybe it was just as well that she had miscarried. Betsy sighed deeply as her reverie was slipping away. It was pointless anyway, going over it in her mind again. Len never mentioned marriage, nor spoke of the baby.

And he was right about the family thing. She couldn't imagine her life now without the circus, without Len, Buster, even Polly, or Rolly Polly as she called herself! The four of them had been there the longest and had been through a lot together. And it truly wasn't a stable or suitable life for a child!

Day II on the Train

The following morning, Betsy woke Joyce up and asked her to join her for breakfast in the dining car. "Leave your things here, Honey. They'll be safe for you till tonight."

While Betsy waited, Joyce slipped out of her nightdress and into her previous day's travelling clothes and followed Betsy to the diner.

She suddenly found herself in the handsomely panelled dining car, trimmed with shiny chrome and bustling with white-jacketed waiters weaving in and out of tables topped with fine linen. She was reminded of her summer holidays at the island and all the finery of the dining room there.

Before she could object, Betsy had prepaid the waiter for both their meals. "We ain't rich, but we do like to start the day right," Betsy declared. Before Joyce could blink an eye, she was enjoying a good portion of oranges, eggs, fried bread, and even a cup of coffee, the first cup she had ever tasted. Although she wasn't sure she enjoyed it, she had nodded and smiled as Betsy poured her a second cup which she sipped without wincing.

"Your Ma ain't here now," said Betsy. "So go on, enjoy yourself! You've still got a long way to go, Honey!"

Boldly, Betsy unfolded a white handkerchief and slipped four pieces of toast inside, along with a few orange sections, refolding it neatly into a square. She then tucked them inside her handbag, as she rose from the table. "C'mon, that'll do for our lunch, Darling."

"I've got a sandwich still left from yesterday," Joyce said timidly. "We can share that as well."

After breakfast, Joyce sat with the entertainers again while they regaled her with stories of their travels and adventures behind the scenes.

"Ya," said the fat lady. (Because she called herself that, she didn't seem to mind.) "D'ya remember that night we was celebratin' old Buster's fortieth, and I started choking on that piece of cake? Must've been something strange in that, 'cause I never met a cake I didn't like before. Well … I liked it, but boy, it sure came back on me! I was makin' very close friends with the toilet mosta that night, remember? Manager Roy was none too pleased with me that week, was he?" She started to howl with laughter. The four rolls of fat on her front rippled and shook as she giggled and shrieked with the hilarity of the thought. The others chuckled along more quietly at the memory of it.

"Then there was the time Lucinda was practising on the 'peze without the belt," Len chimed in. "God, we's all scared outta our minds with her, remember? We told her and told her. Fourteen years old, a mind of a maniac, and a nerve to match, wasn't she? Always wantin' to swing from the top without no safety belt. Thank God she decided to go off with that part-timer we had, 'wise, she wouldn't have lasted till sixteen at that rate!"

Even Raz, the lion tamer, shook his head and closed his eyes as the story was retold.

Joyce could feel the relaxed closeness among the group as she sat contentedly listening, shuddering occasionally at some of the talking points.

After a while, Betsy opened her stolen lunch and Joyce rummaged in her bag for her leftover sandwich. It wasn't much, but they pulled the bread into quarters, and offered it around. Some accepted, others declined. The fat lady laughed and said, "Do I really look to you like I'd survive on a bit of bread for my lunch, Honey?"

Once again, Joyce broke through the protective wall of shyness and laughed with the others. She wanted the tales to go on and on; she was enjoying both the stories and the storytellers so much.

But then suddenly, everything came to a halt when the conductor announced the next stop would be Port Arthur."Ooooh, that's us!" Len grunted and quickly stood up, grabbing Betsy by the elbow.

"Oh, is it already?!" Betsy too had been immersed in the afternoon's storytelling.

"Yep, it is, indeedy! Can't wait to taste that Northern brew they make up here. Yaaahooey!" Len was halfway down the aisle toward the exit door.

With a groan, Betsy jumped up and grabbed her luggage. She had left some things in her upper berth but was always careful to keep her suitcase by her side. With a few brisk hugs for Joyce, and Betsy making her promise to take good care of herself, the circus performers said their goodbyes. And then, like a magic trick involving the whole troupe, they vanished from the carriage.

Had someone already mentioned they were only travelling together for the first night? Joyce couldn't remember. Several long minutes elapsed before she could gather herself again for the next leg of the journey.

She looked out the window to see the shores of Lake Superior. It was a massive expanse of blue. She couldn't even see the other side, as she was used to at Lake Joseph in Muskoka. Large cargo ships were docked in the harbour, and the cold air was broken with cries from gulls. The snowy harbour was busy with workers unloading big containers and fishermen arriving with nets laden with large catches. Alongside the harbour were empty box cars, and ropes and carts, and a few men were hauling fish from the boats and into the cargo cars.

As the train crossed a railway bridge, Joyce could see long flatbed trucks loaded with lengths of fallen trees, as drivers sped along to their destinations. Dark browns, blacks and greys were the colours of the working harbour.

Still, the shimmering lake made a beautiful, dominant backdrop.

Years later in the 1960s, the Gitchi-Gami (the Ojibwe name for Lake Superior) was featured in "The Wreck of the *Edmund Fitzgerald*," crooned by recording artist Gordon Lightfoot. His ballad about the stormy inland sea devouring the *Edmund Fitzgerald* echoed across the waters for years and into the Lakehead harbour. The song became a fitting tribute to lives lost on this and other ships, such as the treasure laden *Gunilda*. Many years later, the twin cities of Port Arthur and Fort William merged and fittingly became known as Thunder Bay.

The staggeringly beautiful view meant Joyce only half noticed the pungent smell, not of freshly caught pickerel and lake trout, but of something else.... Chimney stacks spouted heavy smoke from the paper mills lining the banks of the English-Wabigoon River system. Joyce's family would reflect on that scene years later, in the 1970s, when the polluting legacy dominated the newspaper columns, triggering government inquiries and remedial schemes. It was another cruel attack on the landscape for Native peoples, pushing them away from their natural resources and into the unnatural urban environments.

Second Night

With a heavy sigh, Joyce gathered up her suitcase and trudged back through the train to her original seat. She needed to be back where she started to avoid the loneliness which swamped her after the colourful family of circus entertainers left the train. When she looked once again at the cold corduroy seats though, she realised it wasn't going to be any less lonely. But at least she wouldn't have to share the carriage with any strangers.

She plunked herself down, a strange sensation finding its way to her stomach once again. Although the twelve-year-old was not very fond of reading, Andrew had given her a copy of *Anne of Green Gables* before she left. "You will get to like it, Joyce. You only think about reading in that way now because of your school homework. You'll see, Joyce, reading can be really enjoyable. It will make you forget your problems for a while."

She now found herself wheedling it out of the suitcase and stroking its cover a little before opening it to read the introduction. Then, surprising herself, she quickly became immersed in the story. In fact, it completely absorbed her, and a couple of hours passed by without her noticing. When she looked up, and realised where she was, she conceded that Andrew had been right once again. Reading could be quite nice.

Turning her attention back to the journey, she peered out the window and wondered where they were. She must have missed some stops without noticing. Daylight began to fade, though it was only mid-afternoon. The drama and beauty of the Northern Ontario landscape with its blue lakes and rocky cliffs had disappeared with her colourful friends.

Instead, the land had now flattened out completely, and all she could see outside were endless fields covered in grey snow. In fact, as the daylight dimmed, her view was almost black and white with a bit of brown here and there. She had entered the province of Manitoba, the first of the prairie provinces.

Towering cylindrical grain elevators provided the only vertical break in the horizon. She marvelled at the height of them. She had seen silos before on family farms near her home, but nothing compared to these. And so many of them. The replicated watchtowers guarded the wheatfields, now cleared and barren for approaching winter. Identical to each other, and lining the flat earth, the scene evoked a dull feeling in Joyce. Only occasionally there was a letter or two, large silver G's and E's, breaking the uniformity and marking the top of the elevators.

"That part of the trip may be quite boring, Joyce," Andrew had warned. "It's wheat fields for as far as the eye can see. Just the grain elevators will break it up—huge silos will be the only vertical part of the landscape—pretty well everything else will be horizontal. But then, just think how many loaves of bread they produce. There's enough grain grown in Manitoba and Saskatchewan for the whole of Canada and more for an entire week!"

Now, a third conductor, a bearded man who walked with a slight limp came through the carriage. "Winnipeg, next stop!" Then, seeing her ticket carried on to Edmonton, he patted her shoulder with a little tap. "We've now left the province of Ontario, my Dear. It's the prairies we're into now."

Joyce nodded and said thank you, reflecting, "Yes, Andrew had described them very well."

"Winnipeg, passengers for Winnipeg!" Again the conductor's call startled Joyce from her thoughts. She looked out the window into the empty darkness broken by the twinkle of city lights. For her, the skyline could not be distinguished as a major landmark in her journey. Buildings were rectangular, hard lines were unbroken by other shapes. But was it possible the cold was seeping further into the carriage and up through her seat and they neared Winnipeg? She shivered and pulled her coat tighter around her.

Then, suddenly, a large sign illuminated her view, and the spectacle overtook the chill for a few seconds. "The Royal National Ballet!" Joyce recalled a friend of Marg's having taken dance lessons. The informer of this fact, the sister of the dancer, had added, "If you're lucky you might be invited to the ballet performance at the end of the year. The twelve-year-old remembered how hearing this fact gave her a tingly feeling. It was something unknown to her, and she was in awe. She would have to write to Marg and tell her about the sign.

"Winnipeg is the capital of Manitoba," she thought, shivering. "We have left Ontario, and Manitoba and Saskatchewan are much narrower. They won't take too long to cross, and tomorrow, I should be arriving in Edmonton. Tomorrow, I'll be arriving at Aunt Lorna's house! Suddenly, along with the cold, she found her appetite had made a surprise return.

Table for One

Having been treated by Betsy and then sharing food with the troupe, Joyce realised she still had all her money, and could now have a decent meal in the dining car. And, as she had eaten breakfast there with Betsy, she felt a little more confident about returning for dinner.

Finding more and more courage, she checked the time with a passing employee, who confirmed it was time for the evening sitting. Lumbering along with her suitcase, so that she could then go straight to the sleeping car after dinner, she worked her way to the warm aromas of the diner. There were a few uniformed employees sitting across from each other at two tables, and several fully or partly occupied by about eight or nine suited gentlemen, drinking and talking together. At another table, was the lady she had seen yesterday with her little boy, Billy. She smiled at mother and son, who seemed to be just about finished their meal. It looked as though they both had had some kind of stew, judging from the remnant brown sauce soaking chunks of potato and carrot on the little boy's plate.

Joyce found a free table between the men and the family and sat down.

"Hey, Honey, you can join us," a man sitting with two others called to her. "There's a free seat here!"

Joyce lowered her eyes to the place setting before her and shifted in her seat.

"Just mind your own business," the waiter scolded the older diners, as he appeared to take Joyce's order. The men issued a few small jeers and returned to their drinks and pie.

Reassuring her, the waiter said, "Don't worry, little one, they're only going to Regina, so they'll be getting off soon. They won't be around much longer."

Goodness, that meant she would soon be in Saskatchewan, and two provinces away from her Ontario home!

Too dark to see but accompanying the train on its journey across the plains was the Assiniboine River. A blue garland unfurled, it bobbed evenly alongside the route, splitting the flat horizon. Its bounty of walleye and smelt nourished the prairie population as they worked to harvest the wheat which fed the rest of the land.

In the dining car, there was a small card on the linen tablecloth, stating the menu for the evening meal. There were two options: stewed chicken and vegetables, or shepherd's pie, both at a price Joyce could manage. The choice was easy.

"What can I get you?" the waiter asked politely. A hint of a smile curled around Joyce's lips despite her efforts to keep straight-faced. Her brothers used to joke that the amount of meat in their mother's shepherd's pie depended on how many students their mother had taught that week. The bittersweet memory of the family giggle garnished the prospect of Joyce's evening alone.

"Are you going to Vancouver?" The lady at the next table helped her son up and turned to leave. Billy lurched and moaned a little at her side.

"Uh, oh, thank you, no, I'm going to Edmonton," Joyce stammered awkwardly.

"Oh, that's a shame. You will be leaving the train in the morning, otherwise we could have had dinner together tomorrow evening," said the kindly and patient lady.

"Oh, yes, that would have been very nice."

With a smile, the mother explained that her son was tired and needed to go to bed, so she said goodbye and, supporting the boy's arm, led him out of the dining car.

Saying goodbye, Joyce wished the family could have stayed a little longer to keep her company.

By the time her order arrived, most of the loud men had departed, so Joyce found she could relax a little. The train chugged along, but somehow the dining car seemed to jerk less than her home carriage. Delicately, she tasted the chicken dish, and thought it was delicious, with more meat than she had expected. Included in the dinner was a custard dessert, which Joyce enjoyed as well, despite the solitary nature of her meal. On her own, she could at least eat her dinner at her own pace, rather than feeling rushed or worrying about being scolded. It was a stark contrast from the stiff dinners back home where manners and rules governed the dinner table.

Then, as the last mouthfuls of sweet custard slid off the spoon, she felt an achy feeling in her stomach. Thinking about it, it had been with her off and on all day. It made her even gladder that she had remembered to bring her suitcase with her so she could proceed directly to her berth for the night.

She paid the bill, picked up her suitcase, and headed in the direction of the sleeping cars. Outside, nightfall blackened the windows.

Seemingly, the boldest of the men had lingered in the dining car.

"Hey, Honey, where you off to? It's early yet. Why don't you stay and talk to me a while? It's lonely on these long train trips, don't you think?" Luckily, his chatter was quickly cut following a severe look in his direction from one of the night staff.

Joyce quickened her step out of the carriage and made a beeline for her berth. Discovering with a huge sigh of relief that no one had taken Betsy's place on the bed below her, Joyce hiked herself up onto the berth she had occupied the previous night. She quickly got undressed and under the covers. Almost instantly she fell quickly and deeply asleep as the train trundled along into the night.

Edmonton, Alberta

Lorna cradled her afternoon coffee and studied the oatmeal cookie on the little table at her side. Her wavy hair, silvering around her face, was normally well-groomed and tidy. Today though, it was a little wispy around the edges where she had been running her fingers through it.

She tugged at her wool skirt, as she crossed her legs and breathed a little more deeply. She was cosy and warm in her well-heated home, yet she gave a small shiver, and pulled the pale blue cardigan together around her slight frame. Keeping time with her heartbeat, was her breastbone, which protruded and receded with every breath.

Her china cup clattered a little, breaking the dead silence in the house as she set it down.

Jumping up suddenly, she decided to do another inspection of her spare room. Anxiously, she dashed along the hall, and opened the door to the freshly painted lavender scene. Surveying her work, she dropped her chin with a small nod. She was pleased with the feminine colour scheme she'd chosen. She glanced up with approval at the hand-painted border trimming which danced with yellow primroses and lacey snowdrops. Lorna smiled at the word "border" sounding the same as "boarder."

The new drapes she had chosen in a deep mauve highlighted the soft new tones, and she brushed her long fingers along the satiny window dressings and contrasting sashes. The pale pink appliquéd tulips gave a lovely accent to the room. She pursed her lips in satisfaction. She did hope Joyce would be pleased with her new room and Lorna's choices of decoration. Perhaps she should have waited, but she wanted everything to be new and fresh for her niece's arrival.

Back in the kitchen, she poured herself another drink, and looked out the window at the icy covering which crusted her backyard. She picked up her cup and set it down again, fidgeting and moving a few items along the kitchen countertop. Behind her was a small proverb from Psalm 27:10. "When my father and mother forsake me, then the LORD will take me up." It had been in the family for generations, and on Lorna's wall for years. Unread. Turning her thoughts to her car trip to the train station, she hoped the roads would be kept clear.

"Only a little girl, that's all," she thought, "a young girl after all." She would go to school, come home, there would be homework to do—that would be simple enough. It might be a slightly different curriculum than she had studied in Ontario but that would be no problem. Lorna would help her with her homework, she would enjoy doing that, and that would fill their evenings. After all, she herself had been a good student when she was young, and as she still worked with numbers, mathematics would certainly be no problem. Joyce was her niece, and no doubt she would be a good student too. Isabelle had said that she was a fairly quiet girl, "no trouble really." They would enjoy learning together. It would be a new challenge ... for both of them.

What else did she need to think about? She looked at the calendar. Joyce would be arriving the following day. There was the grocery shopping to be done of course. What would the girl eat? Joyce would eat what was put in front of her, if she knew her sister Isabelle! Joyce would be raised to be polite, and appreciate what she was given, rather than expecting anything different.

Flipping the calendar over, she then wondered about the weekends. What on earth would they do with themselves on the weekends?

There was church, of course, on Sunday. On her own she attended occasionally, not every week. Taking a deeper breath, she smiled to herself, realising she would have to consider being more regular once Joyce arrived!

But Saturdays, what could they do with Saturdays? What did she do now on her own? After the food shopping, she spent most Saturdays at the library. Lorna never needed the full three-week borrowing period to finish her stack of books; she went through them within the week, returning and carefully selecting more. Biographies were her favourite genre. She preferred non-fiction in general, but she sometimes read historical novels as well, just for something lighter. She wondered if Joyce liked reading.

What did a twelve-year-old girl do? In her letter, her sister hadn't really written anything much at all about Joyce's own interests. The little girl played the piano, of course. Isabelle had taught her, and she had already taken some exams at the Royal Conservatory. "Damn!" Lorna hadn't even considered her niece's musical education. She should already have bought a piano and had it waiting for Joyce when she arrived. Unless maybe she would like to take up another instrument. Except ... who would teach her? Lorna was the only one of the females in the family who didn't play an instrument. She was always more interested in books and travelling.

"It's difficult to carry a piano with you on a long trip!" The thought gave rise to a short chuckle.

Goodness, it was hard to imagine that it had been over thirty-five years since she herself had left home as a teenager to launch her career in finance. Was it really that long ago?

It always seemed to Lorna that she was a little different from her nine brothers and sisters, and that somehow, she was not really a full-fledged member of the family. As she grew up in Ontario, she had always longed to live somewhere else— somewhere new. In fact, she had been very lucky, as the work she had done as a young woman on the ships as a bursar had not only provided some great professional experience, but it had also given her some incredible adventures.

Lorna had spent the first ten years of her working life exploring the exotic treasures of most of the other continents. From the Cape of Good Hope at the tip of Africa to Cape Horn which skirted South America, to the hypnotic coastal views of India, she had likely seen more of the world than most of her family and friends combined. Initially at least, her career offered her a life which was the stuff of dreams. But ultimately, she longed to settle somewhere. Funny, how the Rockies, those stunning, rugged mountains, which crested the coast of her home country, had begun to beckon her home. It was thousands of miles from her family. Yet once she arrived in Edmonton, she immediately felt she had come home.

But how long had it been now since she had moved into her cottage outside the city ... all on her own. Had it been nearly twenty-five years?

Well, not counting the time she spent with Richard. And even that was ... about eighteen years ago. He was ... she would have ... followed him just about anywhere ... but, she hardly thought of him now. The craziness of it all, the carefree times, the ridiculous shrillness of her laughter, his tender caress ... the ... baby ... the child they had lost.

She must have had a fit of madness to have gotten involved with Rhonda's boss. Lorna and Richard had only worked together for a few months when his eyes started to linger a little too long on her hands when she came into his office to do some work for him in Rhonda's absence one week. When she handed the figures over to him, she felt an electricity in her hips like nothing she had ever experienced before.

Lorna assumed he was married; there were photos of young children on his desk, although not of his wife. Rhonda then explained that he was actually a widower, and, she had noted, a devoted father. It added to the attraction for Lou (as he always called her), although not his availability. She would never want to interfere with anyone's family commitments. She had always felt strongly that children should come first in a person's life.

In any case, she had never been one just to go for the handsome face and sturdy shoulders. There had to be something more, an indescribable attraction to their soul. Throughout her life that feeling didn't come about often.

In fact, she had always thought she would stay single; she was not really "the marrying type." Lorna was a strong enough character not to care about being labelled an "old maid" or a "dried-up, old spinster." She was a career person anyway.... Well, okay, she was working as a secretary to the finance director at present, but even at her age, she still had dreams, ambitions of working her way up in the company, becoming a department manager, maybe even working on client development.

That was the only regret she had really ... about Richard ... losing her job. Obviously, she was devastated about losing the baby, nothing could compare to that pain, but that wasn't anyone's fault. She realised that it was just not meant to be. But did she deserve to be "quietly disappeared" from the company, while he stayed on to rise to positions of grandeur?

It was so unfair that because women carried the children it was obvious if they were pregnant and unmarried. How life would be different if men who fathered children outside of marriage developed some dramatic physical change as evidence! Wouldn't that be a more balanced consequence for both women and men? Why are women always paying so dearly for nature's brutal design.

However, Lorna was never one to dwell on her misfortunes for any length of time. In fact, thinking about it, that was one way in which she did resemble the rest of the family. All of them had been raised to "carry on regardless," to "keep a stiff upper lip," and this was a lesson in life that she was always glad she had learned.

Lorna pressed her lips together. She did love working for Alberta Life. It was an insurance company whose ethos she could support, and even perhaps in time, become passionate about.

Her life now followed a straight path really.… Her writing sat neatly on the blue lines of her notepaper; her grammar followed the rules. Even her long, ranch-style home was rectangular, and thinking about it, her tables and chairs were pretty squarely aligned as well! It all made her life simple, clean, and easy.

Nowadays, she lived life pretty much within society's margins (margins were also straight lines, thinking about it!) She didn't stray much beyond her work life, a bit of church, the library, and one or two friends, including Rhonda, who had been there when her life fell apart. Rhonda was always reminding her that life goes on, and it could still be fun. Lorna admitted she herself had a tendency to be too serious.

The two of them would meet on weekends, go out for dinner and sometimes a show afterwards—when they weren't too late for the theatre or movie. Sometimes their chats got so intense that they had forgot the time. The two of them could talk for hours on almost any subject. Sometimes Lou admitted to feeling a little tender after their evenings together. But then Ronda was happily married and with a young son. Although Lou had never been the jealous sort, she occasionally allowed herself a slip of envy over her friend's full life.

In any case, it was important to Lou to keep up with Rhonda and hoped she could continue the friendship after her niece's arrival, even if their "girls' nights" would have to take a back seat for now. Anyway, Lorna had plenty of questions for her friend about being a mother, or at least some guidelines on raising a young child.

Lorna was the second eldest of ten, and her sister Isabelle was the youngest girl. They were separated not only by large stretches of wheatfields, towns, trees, roads, lakes and rocks, but by nearly twenty years in age. Lorna was now nearly 58, and Isabelle was still in her thirties. Thinking about it, the last time she had seen Isabelle, Joyce had not been much more than a baby. Since then, Isabelle had had two more children. Boys again! Lorna had never even met the younger ones, and with Joyce coming to stay, Isabelle would be left with an all-male cast at home. It was going to be ruddy hard work for her sister now that her scoundrel husband had left! Men, sometimes! And leaving a wife with four boys and one poor girl! Well ... four boys now at least for the next two years! But ... she must focus on her own tasks at hand. She just couldn't believe she had a child coming to live with her after all this time!

Day III on the Train

Joyce woke up early. Her first sensation was of being in darkness—it was not even sunrise yet. The second was being wet. She needed the toilet—in a hurry. She felt soaked between her legs. Yet how could she be? Goodness, she was old enough not to wet herself!

Everything on this train felt different though, even her skin. A sour smell was wafting around her berth. Sitting up, she lifted the blankets up to slide her legs to the floor. Under her, blood pooled on the sheets. It seemed to be coming from her, from Joyce ... from between her legs!

Horrified and confused, her thoughts raced and clashed into each other! What to do? Frantically, she rummaged around the berth, and as quietly and swiftly as possible, she lifted herself into a sitting position. Then she found some handkerchiefs in her luggage and managed to soak up the strange scarlet flow between her legs. But what was already soaked through to the mattress left a menacing crimson stain. Terrified of being seen in such a state, she tucked her nightdress in and around her legs, pulled on her housecoat, snatched her clothing into a tight fist, and awkwardly stepped onto the edge of the bottom bunk, praying no one was asleep there, and slid onto the floor of the moving train.

The bottom berth was thankfully empty, and now she hoped the carriages were as well.

Stick icicles were her arms. Her legs, only slightly fatter, were no warmer. Jostling against the berths, petrified of others, she shuffled along the aisle, as quickly and as quietly as possible, while grabbing at whatever she could for support. She prayed she was the first one up on the entire train.

As fast as she dared, she got to the toilet and knocked and banged on the door to check it was unoccupied. An eternity of waiting yielded no reply so she rushed in, pulled down her bloomers as fast as she could, and squatted on the toilet. "Never sit," mother had said. "Always hover for hygiene's sake."

With her stomach heaving drily, she watched a bloody stream join her pee in the bowl. What was it? She was dying on this trip.

The crotch of her bloomers was bloody and more seemed to be pouring from her. Everything looked red under her in the dark cubicle. What was happening to her? Why was she bleeding from "down there" of all places?

Joyce shuddered and started to shake. Terror winning over the cold she felt, she fumbled across to the porcelain bowl to find some soap. After a few more clumsy movements, she managed to wash some of the blood from her legs, and basin, removed her nightdress and reclaimed her housecoat. Frantically, she scoured the toilet with a clean handkerchief, which she then stowed in the small garbage pail provided and slipped back out into the darkened corridor. Not yet daybreak, she was relieved to find no light was shining through the train windows as yet.

Arriving back at her berth, the twelve-year-old hiked herself up onto the upper bed again. Silently she struggled out of the bloody bloomers and into a clean pair from her suitcase. But their bleached white gusset was soon spotted with blood. "Make it stop, please, please make it stop. She lay back against the pillow and closed her eyes with fear.

Joyce thought of her prayer book and the lessons there, but she dared not fumble around the berth anymore lest someone hear her. "Ours is a vengeful God." Mother said it meant God punished people for wrongdoing.

What had she done? She must have done something—likely lots of things. Firstly, she must have done something to upset her father, as he had left. Maybe that was really her fault. That was why she was being sent away. That was her punishment, and now she was bleeding. Her Aunt Sadie had told her once that if they would have all behaved better, their father wouldn't have gone away. And if her father hadn't gone away, there would have been more money for the family, Joyce knew. Maybe then she wouldn't have been sent away.

Mother often did seem to be angry with her no matter what she did. Her brothers never seemed to get blamed for anything. Well, except Andrew of course. At her house, the eldest son and the only daughter always seemed to be the ones at fault.

Was she bleeding to death because she had done something bad at home? Her father leaving was the start of the family falling apart. Perhaps she was now being punished by death.

The day her father left, she felt she would never see him again. Then when she boarded the train—Had it really only been two days ago?—she felt sure she would never see her mother and brothers again. And now, with the bleeding, she knew it to be true.

Exhaustion took the hand of the bleeding, and somehow the pre-daylight hours were overtaken by more slumber.

Suddenly, Joyce was shaken awake by the conductor's announcement. "Medicine Hat, anyone for Medicine Hat?"

Medicine Hat. Forgetting the blood for a few seconds, Joyce's brain swirled between humour and seriousness. Was there really such a place? Then, reality reared its cruel head, and Joyce was mired in confusion. Was she dreaming? Was there such a place?

Joyce would later learn that Medicine Hat was an English interpretation of Saamis (SA-MUS), the Blackfoot word for the eagle tail feather headdress worn by medicine men. She also learned that several legends are associated with the name of a mythical mer-man river serpent named Soy-yee-daa-bee—the Creator—who appeared to a hunter and instructed him to sacrifice his wife to get mystical powers which were manifest in a special hat. Another legend told of a battle long ago between the Blackfoot and the Cree in which a retreating Cree "Medicine Man lost his headdress in the South Saskatchewan River.

"MEDicine Hat," the call came again, now more insistently, and Joyce sat up. It was a place. Medicine—that must be what she needed—perhaps she should get off here! No one else seemed to be.

For a few serene seconds, she had had no problems. But she had now remembered her blood-stained undercarriage, and shame soaked her entire body. She struggled into her clothes and out of the berth, trying her best to conceal the stained bedding, and clutching her suitcase, swung her legs over the side of the berth and with a quick step from the lower bed, stepped into the aisle.

Her hair was snarled and matted against her white face, but she hurried from the sleeping cars to escape the night's evidence. She would make her way to the toilet, and try to wash herself again, then go back to her original seat.

With relief, most of the carriages were still fairly empty, as presumably other passengers were at breakfast, but passing through the dining car, she kept her gaze down at her feet.

From the corner of her eye, she could see the taunting men from the night before, but they made no remarks now. Then the friendly lady with the young son spotted her and called to her. "Oh, hello, again, are you—"

Joyce's only reply was a nod and a bolt. She didn't want to linger a second longer than was necessary to travel through the car.

Finding the toilet again, she stumbled into the cramped space with her suitcase. Then, lifting her skirt, she tucked it under her chin and dragged down her bloomers again to inspect them. They were saturated.

In a flurry of urgency, she unravelled the spool of toilet paper, folded it several times and stuffed it into the gusset of her bloomers. She had just enough time to wash her hands before someone was knocking on the door for their turn. Terror and confusion entered first. Fumbling to pull her clothing together as fast as she could, she slipped into the corridor where a man was waiting. He made no comment as she rushed past him.

Outside, daylight was breaking through and the polite foothills of Alberta rolled gently by unnoticed.

Arrival in Edmonton

After checking her fuel gauge, and looking at all the clocks in the house, Lorna prepared to leave for the train station. She calculated she had at least an hour to spare before Joyce's train arrived. The weather and snow plows had teamed up after yesterday's snowfall and her route was clear with only tiny stars of ice dazzling her vision along the roads.

As she drove, she realised her stomach felt tight. How ludicrous that was! True enough, it was going to be a huge change in both their lives with Joyce coming to live with her. But, hopefully, it would be a lovely experience for them both.

She decided she wouldn't overwhelm the girl by embracing her when she first arrived. It wasn't appropriate. They really didn't know each other yet. She would give her a chance to settle in first before showing too much affection. There was plenty of time for that.

Under her heavy winter coat, she was wearing one of her favourite green print dresses. Somehow, it helped her feel a little younger than her years. With her smart forest green hat and matching gloves, she felt warm and ever so slightly stylish as she pulled into the station parking lot. Spotting a space, she pulled into it.

Then, checking the time on the clock that crowned the station roof, she realised there was still plenty of time before Joyce arrived.

In the distance, blue and pink hues were taking turns on the steep slopes of the Rockies. To adorn their November season, luscious frosty lashings slithered down the snowy peaks. A temptation never indulged, Lorna thought of Richard's love of skiing, and issued a small sigh. Perhaps Joyce might like to try it ... if it were affordable.

She decided to allow herself a few minutes rest and closed her eyes. Forty minutes later, she found herself jolting awake with a start. She could hear a departure being announced. Taking a deep breath, she opened her door, slid her long legs out of the car, and rubbed her hands together in anticipation.

Feeling a little more confident now, the lady of the west wore a hopeful expression as she strode through the station. More arrivals and departures were being announced. Perhaps the train had come in early. Lorna moved through the building to the designated platform. She craned her long neck, searching to get sight of her young niece.

Suddenly, she realised Isabelle had not even described the girl to her. The last time she had seen a photograph of her, Joyce had been about five years old. She was very fair then, so presumably she would still be blonde. Longer hair perhaps. Where was she? Had Isabelle described HER to Joyce?

Being so tall herself, Lorna thought she should be able to spot the twelve-year-old with no trouble. The train was in station, but she was surprised by the throng standing in wait.

Joyce disembarked and stood still amid the confusion on the platform. Blurry eyes met a slur of announcements filling her ears. Confusion mounted as people shouted to descending passengers.

"Roger, Roger!"

"Francis, Emily, Emil— over here!"

Then, suddenly there was a firm grip on her elbow, and she turned to find her aunt Lou putting her arm around her shoulders. As Joyce's head lifted toward her new guardian, tears leaked from her eyes, triumphing over polite reserve. Joyce gave one loud choke before being folded into her aunt's arms.

"Ah, Joyce! I'm so, so pleased to … see you! What's the … oh, please, don't cry … two years will fly by, you'll see … and you'll soon be back home with your mother. Please, please don't worry."

Then a vague notion of something amiss, floated into the older woman's brain. Difficult news unspoken. The young girl looked worryingly pale.

"Oh-oh-oh, you poor, poor dear." Come on, let's get you home to your bed as quickly as we can. The car is just over here. Are you feeling a little unwell?"

As she bundled her shivering niece into the car, the icy mountains stood watch. Lorna's first thoughts were that the poor girl needed a warmer coat, winter clothing. She would organize a shopping trip as soon as possible.

As she started the engine, Lorna hoped Joyce would be warmer in the car. She wheeled around and out of the parking lot before saying, "What is it, Joyce? You do look quite pale."

"I-I, y-yes, n-no thank you, I-I-I'm sorry I'm not well, but … I-I-I'm sorry … I'm dying, you know."

Edmonton Home

Lorna reassured her niece all the way home that she was not dying, that she could promise her on the Bible in fact that she was not dying, and that all young girls had this happen and it was just part of growing up. Her niece, staying mostly silent after a brief explanation as to her "illness," looked small and terrified on the car seat as she sped along as quickly as possible.

Once through the door at home, Lorna took Joyce calmly but firmly by the hand, found a wedge of cotton in the cupboard (which thankfully she had kept there without even thinking of poor Joyce) and some safety pins, and led her to her new bedroom. She laid the towelling on the bed, sat down, and beckoned Joyce to sit next to her, and explained how to fast the cotton into her bloomers to absorb the flow.

"The flow?" Joyce was shaking terribly. "It won't stop?"

"It normally lasts five days to a week, depending. Everyone is different. It comes once a month, Dear.... I'm so sorry this started while you were on the train, but you're not to worry. I had periods, your mother has periods, we all—all us girls have periods until you're older like I am. You have a wash, and once you have yourself cleaned up and sorted with the pad, come downstairs and I'll explain everything to you, dear. There is nothing to worry about at all. We'll chat it through properly when you're ready. All right?"

The older woman added that she was very surprised that her mother had not mentioned this natural process of becoming a woman nor explained to Joyce about monthly periods. She and all her sisters had them. All young women had them! It was wonderful really, just a sign of growing up and becoming a woman.

"Does this happen to you every month?" Voicing her question aloud now, the twelve-year-old was incredulous.

"N-no not now, not anymore. I'm too old now. My periods stopped a few years ago now. But I had them every month for over 40 years!" (Well, she thought privately except during pregnancy ...)

Wordlessly, Joyce nodded feebly. Lorna then hugged her warmly and with a firm pat on her hand went downstairs to prepare some tea.

"What? Monthly?" Joyce wondered silently. "This happens to everyone every month?" On hearing this, she contemplated whether she wouldn't rather have been dying, as she thought was happening, than go through this every month.

Downstairs, Lorna bustled around the kitchen more noisily than usual. What a welcome! Poor Joyce. Poor, poor child! Lorna had been absolutely flabbergasted that Isabelle hadn't spoken to Joyce about menstruation!

"That poor, poor little girl. She was only a child! Well, certainly she was an adolescent. She looked to weigh about 70 pounds or so! But twelve years old! All alone on that train and starting her periods for the first time! And she had no idea, no idea at all! Of course she would think that she was dying! What a terrible start to her time away from home!"

She had to admit though, she herself hadn't given any thought to Joyce's changing young body and the possibility of her starting her periods just yet. It must have been brought on by the journey and her nervousness about travelling on the train and leaving home for years!

Joyce was still shaking when she came downstairs and it took Lorna a while longer to get Joyce to calm down and to take in the science lesson that Lorna, ill prepared, was forced to present to her niece.

The twelve-year-old choked back a few dry sobs and sat shaking on the couch for quite a while. Lorna put her arm around her and rocked her a little until she grew quiet. In a trial by fire, the aunt in training had to calm Joyce down and gently explain what was actually happening to her body. She even felt she had to touch on "the facts of life" to the poor thing—she had no idea, no idea at all!

Lorna felt angry with her sister for not properly preparing her daughter for this next stage of life. No doubt Isabelle had lectured her endlessly on her manners, keeping quiet on the train, how much she should spend, and on and on. But not the most important development in her daughter's life! The older sister had spent only moments with her niece, yet she noticed that the young girl's chest was starting to swell a little. There were already some hints that she was developing. Really! Couldn't Isabelle have thought a bit more about it, and how sudden changes in routine can stimulate menstruation?

When Joyce joined her again in the kitchen, Lorna got her new charge to eat a little of the lunch she had prepared for her. The older woman worked at pretending to be nonchalant. Satisfied though, that Joyce now understood what was happening not only in her body, but in the bodies of all women, her niece seemed to be feeling a little better.

Lorna then decided it best to carry on with the plans she had made for Joyce's first day. Checking the time was still early afternoon, Lorna took her playfully by the hand once again and took her on a little tour, first of the house which would be her new home, and then, donning their outdoor clothing, of the small, surrounding suburb.

When they returned to the house, Joyce seemed fairly calm, and Lorna suggested she have a short rest before suppertime. Joyce went upstairs to her new bedroom, and after checking herself for leakages lay down on the bed. It was far too much to think about: There was being in a new place. There was bleeding every month for the rest of her life—or nearly! What a life a girl had to endure!

In the quiet of the living room, the older woman took a few deep breaths to compose herself. She refused to hold onto her anger toward her younger sister for very long. There was no point. She felt sure Isabelle had tried to do her best for her daughter, and in any case, the mother of five would have had so much on her mind before Joyce left. It was just sad that she probably had only thought of her as her daughter, not as a young girl growing up in the world.

School in Edmonton

Although she generally thought it best to keep Joyce busy and get into a routine as quickly as possible, Lorna had suggested Joyce wait a couple of days after she arrived before starting at her new school.

"You've had a long, difficult journey, and also … What about starting school on Monday, the first day of the week?"

She'd arrived on a Thursday, and Lorna had a lot of trouble sleeping that night, restless with worry over Joyce. The girl must have been so frightened on that train, and to have her first period present itself under those conditions would have been terrible! She must give her a lot of reassurance without being too overprotective. For her part, Joyce had reported sleeping well, no doubt the result of the exhausting journey and physical changes in her body, and perhaps aided by the two extra hours time change between Ontario and Alberta.

Friday was spent giving Joyce a tour of some of the Rockies. "Where we live is actually some distance from the mountains, you see. They can't actually be seen from our house." Joyce noticed her aunt's use of the pronoun "we."

"That one's called Robson Mountain, and there's a hiking trail leading to the top. Perhaps in the summer holidays we can organise a trip up there."

Joyce's blue eyes widened as she quietly took in the majesty of it all. Lorna was truly grateful the dramatic scenery, with its snowy caps and distinctive hues of blue and pink, seemed to absorb her young niece and evoked several gasps and even a "wow" or two.

Lorna restrained herself from suggesting skiing might be an interest in the future, preferring to let Joyce develop her own ideas.

Then it was a trip into the city—and finding Joyce a new coat. She found her niece almost as shy about shopping as she was about her changing body. But after visiting a few stores, she convinced Joyce to try on a red single-breasted lined coat with a hood. "It looks splendid on you, Joyce! It sets off your blonde hair beautifully too!"

Besides distracting her new young charge from her problems, she very much wanted her to have a feel for life in the west. As they toured around the shops, with their cowboy hats and boots and western gear, the aunt-in-training even prised a little laugh out of Joyce as she tried on a cowboy hat and pretended to shoot the mannequin with her finger.

However, it was the cultural side of life in Edmonton that really absorbed Lorna and she hoped her niece would begin to enjoy it as well. Smiling down at her blonde-haired charge with quick affection, they walked around the centre of the city with its new shops, theatres, churches and even a concert hall.

Joyce nodded with apparent interest in the descriptions she was given of all the city landmarks. Still, she was mostly quiet throughout the day, only responding politely when spoken to. This was no surprise to Lorna of course, but she did hope that Joyce would start to relax and settle in.

Not wanting to probe and prod too much, Lorna decided to ask just a question or two. "Edmonton is a much younger city than Toronto, Joyce. There are lots of new things opening up here, like restaurants, theatres and movie houses. Do you like going to see movies?"

"I've only ever seen one. I went once with my friend Marg. We went to see *Gone with the Wind*."

"Oh, yes, wasn't that an amazing film?"

"Yes, we liked it. It was just .. a bit long."

Lorna gave a little chuckle. It was so wonderful to hear her niece offer an opinion, rather than just politely agreeing with everything. Hopefully it was a small sign she was feeling more comfortable with her.

"We'll have to get the programme some time to see if there are any others you might like to see," Lorna suggested.

As the afternoon light began to fade, the newly acquainted relatives strode toward the parking lot. Inside the car it all grew quiet again, and Lorna began to reflect on the fact that Joyce wasn't just away from her family, she of course had left her friends behind as well. She then asked Joyce a little about her friend Marg and hoped her niece would easily make new friends at school.

On Saturday, Lorna asked Joyce if she would like to go to the library, find out about a membership and possibly see if there were any books she would like to borrow. Joyce had mentioned to her aunt that she had brought *Anne of Green Gables* with her and had started reading that. The parallel in the story to Joyce's own experience was not lost on Lorna.

"Oh, I like the Anne stories. There are others you know, *Anne of Avonlea*, etc, but see how you like that one first, ok? What other things do you like to read?"

"I don't know yet. I've really only just started reading outside of what I have to do for school."

Lorna had to laugh again. She was always glad when Joyce gave honest answers, rather than trying to please her all the time.

The librarian took some details down, and a junior library card was quickly produced for Joyce which she seemed pleased about. As the paperwork was being completed, the librarian suggested she might like to read *The Secret Garden*, published a few years earlier, but instead, Lorna steered Joyce toward some adventure stories aimed at her age group, and her young niece was soon quickly absorbed in reading the jackets of *Tom Sawyer* and *Huckleberry Finn*. Before checking out the books, Lorna breezed through the biography section, delighted to find *A Passage to India* and *The New Negro*, which she checked out for herself.

On the way home, Joyce told her aunt about meeting the Negro conductor on the train and how he had been very kind. Smiling, Lorna then chatted a bit about her experiences in Africa and how she had learned so much from her travels.

The newly acquainted family members grew quiet again during the car journey. Then came Joyce's question: "Did you know about periods before you first went away?"

"Yes, Dear, I didn't leave home until I was nineteen, you see ... and at least I had an older sister, which unfortunately you've missed out on, having all those brothers! Don't worry, we'll mark a little calendar in your room when yours is due. We'll be prepared with plenty of supplies. You'll soon grow used to it and gradually, you won't really think about it too much."

Joyce didn't particularly want to think about it at all, but she was glad to have her aunt to speak to about things.

In the privacy of her room each night, Joyce liked to open her top drawer and look at some of her belongings from home. Unwrapping her music medal from the bit of newspaper she used to protect it, Joyce gingerly laid the gold medallion on the bed. She also had a tiny bottle of perfume, which her Aunt Ida had given her to take on her journey. She dared not open it yet. Her mother had said she was too young to wear perfume anyway. But she lifted the golden top which plugged the special scent and took just a hint of a sniff. She hoped her nostrils weren't making it evaporate. Better than the perfume was the smell of Billy's toy bear. She inhaled its furry babyish aroma. It was Billy.

Her letter from her mother, although a kind of scolding, was still precious to her, and she spread it out over her blankets, not always to read it but just to touch it. She hadn't noticed it before, but on the back of the letter, was a quotation from Psalm 91:11. "For He will command his angels to guard you in all your ways." Joyce thought of the little plaque on the wall in her mother's kitchen. She had memorised it without realising it. "But I am ever with you; you have taken me by my right hand ..."

Isabelle

Sitting in the dim evening light, Isabelle took off her spectacles and pinched the bridge of her nose. They had already needed to be replaced nine times in her lifetime. She had been wearing glasses since she was three years old, and for all of the 35 years since she had loathed them.

She remembered back to the day she played her first piano recital just before her fourth birthday. Her glasses were perched on her nose and stayed there until the end of her piece, when they slipped off and rattled onto the floor as she bowed for the audience. The spectators then broke into loud applause, but Isabelle thought they were laughing at her and raced off the stage.

Reflecting for a few quiet minutes, she thought how she'd never really felt young. It seemed almost from the cradle that she was grownup and taking responsibility. Although she had older sisters and brothers, somehow a lot of the chores at home seemed to fall to her. Someone always seemed to be ill or working so she had been assigned clean-up and laundry duties from a very young age. Sighing heavily with a slight snort, she thought how she was not even 40 yet, but she felt like she was over the hill.

She tugged at the girdle around her middle and shifted her garters a little. Why did women wear so many things that dug into their flesh? Squinting into the twilight, she wondered whether Andrew had actually gone to bed. She hadn't heard him say good night, but he was probably very tired as well. Perhaps she was harder on him than she should be, and maybe naming him after his father didn't help. Damn her so-called husband anyway! He'd only thought of himself, never his family. She didn't mind so much not being a wife anymore, but the children minded very much not having a father around. He didn't even bother to visit them! Just sent the occasional bit of money and half-hearted note.

That was it, anyway. She was finished with him, finished with marriage and finished with men. When Joyce was old enough she'd warn her off them for life as well!

It was hard to believe her eldest was nearly eighteen, and how she wished she could afford to send him to university. Not only couldn't she afford it, she couldn't even afford to think about it!

How hard things have become now. Money was tight, though improved somewhat since the arrival of the two lodgers. It was hard to know if the boys would be able to finish their education. As it was, she was struggling to pay the bills and feed her family. But sending Joyce off to Lou's in Edmonton—over two thousand miles away—that wasn't difficult. It was damned well devastating. She hated herself for it. Unequivocally hated herself! It was the hardest thing she had ever done. But she just had no choice. No choice whatsoever. And she couldn't even bring herself to explain it to Joyce in clear terms. It was just too painful.

The little advertisement she had placed in the local classifieds last month had yielded seven respondents. Three of them she did not invite for an interview. Two were only Andrew's age, so they were clearly out of the question. They had obviously left school at fifteen or sixteen, and there was no chance she would like that kind of influence on her own boys. The third one had a car and had asked if he could park it in front of the house. She didn't like that idea either, in case he had ideas of bringing "visitors" home with him.

In the end, it came down to two candidates, Mr. Randolph Griffiths and Michael Sharp. Mr. Griffiths was single, worked at the local printing company, and always walked to work. This meant he had the money to pay the rent, was jolly enough, and seemed pleased to have a room in a family house. There was something a little different about him that Isabelle couldn't quite work out, but one couldn't have everything, and in any case, it was not her place to ask too many personal questions. He would take Joyce's old room, and with having his evening meal with the family, that would bring in an extra ten dollars a week. That would certainly help to stretch the food budget!

She had felt absolutely treacherous redecorating Joyce's room so that it was suitable for a man. The sashes on the curtains had to go. There were the curly-cued moldings on the dresser that were far too feminine. She exchanged the bureau for one she had out in the woodshed. A little cleaning up, and it was good as new. At first, she thought that she would visit Joyce's dresser regularly in the woodshed, but she never found the time. And perhaps as the saying went, she should remember the least said, soonest mended.

So that took care of Joyce's room. But Mr. Griffith wasn't exactly young; he must have been in his fifties at least. What if something happened to him, and before she knew it, she would have lost her income. Besides, she really wanted to say yes to Michael Sharp. He was a divorced police officer, much younger than herself, with two young boys who lived with their mother nearby. And he needed to find a place to stay quite quickly. She would feel safe having him there. He would definitely be honest—he was a police officer after all! Presumably he would be a disciplined sort as well. He would probably stay for a while to boot. Being newly divorced, he might not be able to afford a place of his own for a bit.

She let her thoughts "percolate" as she called it. Let them bubble through until they, like the coffee, distill into a strong brew.

She began to consider that it was time Billy had his own room, rather than staying in with her. But sharing with David wouldn't work. Billy was going on three and David was eleven going on fourteen. He was far too grownup for Billy's childish ways. Then, suddenly "she smelled the coffee."

She had the answer. Andrew and Robert would have to move in together.

"What? What do you mean!? "You must be joking, Mother! We can't share a room—Robert makes too much noise!"

"Andrew always has his nose in a book," Robert added. "Just not possible." Isabelle couldn't help but chuckle as she already could imagine their loud objections, imagine every protest possible, before she even broached the subject. But again, she really had no choice. The family needed the extra money.

In the end, they decided to convert the upstairs storage cupboard into a room for Robert. She was not happy about it. There was no natural light and with all his football things there was hardly room for Robert. But he insisted that he was happy to sleep in there, especially as he was outside most of the time anyway. "And I'll soon be away at university," he added, characteristically carefree—possibly even a bit insensitive.

Besides, Isabelle felt strongly that two lodgers would be much better than one. Apart from the extra money, they would be a bit of company for one another, rather than being the odd man out sitting at the table amongst the family.

The first meal they shared together was quite an experiment. She'd made one of her signature dishes: meat pies, grinding the leftover roast beef—of which there was precious little—and adding plenty of onion and gravy, cooking it over medium heat and stirring it into one of her homemade pie shells. With mashed potatoes and carrots on the side to flesh it out, and plenty of bread, it made for quite a spread.

To keep the boys in line, she insisted they address the two lodgers as Mr. Griffiths and Mr. Sharp, though it was hard for her to refer to the latter one in the formal, as she was sure he must be at least nine years her junior.

Mr. Griffiths seemed happy with the pie, ate a modest amount of potatoes, and stabbed a few carrots for good measure. Michael, on the other hand, seemed to eat as much as her two teenagers combined. "That was lovely. Is there any more, Mrs. Kelsey?"

"You haven't left much for us," Robert piped up.

"Robert! Please—quiet at the table," Isabelle, embarrassed, admonished him. "Of course, we have plenty more." Thank goodness she'd made a second pie! That wouldn't help the budget stretch very far though. Oh well, this was only the first meal. From tomorrow, she would put up a little sign saying, "Second helpings, 50 cents." She hated the idea, but she would have to be careful to survive.

Within about a week, she found that the new residents had quickly settled in. They didn't seem to bat an eyelash at the house rules, which was a blessing. With everyone's work and school schedules, the rejigged household seemed to bed down very smoothly into a new rhythm as host to the new and old residents. Generally, everyone seemed to be happy enough.

The older boys behaved themselves a little more with an older man as well as a police officer under their roof, which was a bonus. Not that Andrew was ever a problem anyway. Both David and Andrew seemed to find talking points with Mr. Griffiths, who enjoyed discussing history with them and current events. The new tenant engaged with them each evening about which political party was dealing with the economy effectively. Meanwhile, Michael and Robert would play catch in the yard if Mick was home prior to an evening or night shift. Robert seemed to look forward to doing that, asking when Mr. Sharpe would be home again. This seemed to have a calming effect, and she noticed Robert was a bit gentler indoors with his younger brothers especially.

Billy of course was content just playing or being read to. Michael was very good with him too, himself a father of two small boys. Isabelle counted herself as very fortunate to have found two such engaging boarders.

One thing surprised her though. She noticed that Michael preferred to sit opposite Mr. Griffiths at the dinner table, rather than joining his fellow newcomer on the same side of the table. This was a little puzzling, but perhaps being so much younger, he preferred the company of the boys.

The depression meant everyone seemed to be more grateful for what they had, and Isabelle felt pleased and relieved at how things were working out. Anyway, she was too busy just trying to survive and look after her six charges to have much spare time to dwell on Joyce's absence for too long.

She told herself she must make a note on the calendar when it was time to write to Joyce again.

New School Life

Joyce's school back in Toronto was a red-bricked multistorey; a friendly face with oblong Georgian windows for eyes and a wide-mouthed hooded door which welcomed her and her classmates each morning.

By contrast, the modern grey building in Edmonton was long and rectangular, with sports fields on two sides and a paved area which was fenced in on the third. In front, was a driveway and a flat, square entrance. It looked like a "kind of storage facility" was how Aunt Lou described it en route. "But it's brand new, has lots of new books, young, well-trained teachers, sports fields and even your own library and kitchens for home economics." Aunt Lou was enthused as she drove Joyce to school for her first day.

At the mention of "home ec." Joyce thought cooking was the last thing on her mind. She had already had a lot of education in that. Her mother, it seemed, cooked not only almost all day but all evening as well, working to feed the family with meals costing as little as possible. She had a way of making a dish last three days.

Often, one of her brothers would ask Andrew if he knew what they were having for dinner. "Guess," he'd say.

"I don't know, tell me," they'd protest.

"All right, I'll give you a clue," Andrew would tease. "What did we have yesterday and the day before?" Groans would fill the air. "There then, you already know the answer!"

Her mother was a housewife. Well ... without the husband now. If she wasn't cooking, she was cleaning or going to the market, or mending something, or teaching music of course. Yet despite being the only daughter, Joyce had had no interest at all in the domestic side of things. When music filled the house, that was all right. Although a lot of it seemed to be rather serious and heavy, unlike the fun things she heard Buster play on the train.

Inside the geometric building, her new home form teacher welcomed her formally, and showed her to a seat. "You can sit next to Martha here. Martha, you'll make Joyce welcome, won't you." Martha neither smiled nor frowned. A few boys twittered a few giggles, and Joyce noticed the children were dressed much more informally here. Would she be allowed to wear trousers to school like some of the girls were doing?

Fortunately, the teacher did not call on her when she asked the class to answer her questions, and for Joyce, the first day passed in a blur. The teacher was talking, reminding, scolding, praising, comparing and warning all her students, and thankfully, her classmates raised their hands and answered questions.

At recess time, she went outside with Martha, as instructed. Then, as soon as they got outside, Martha said, "Ok, you can just watch us playing ball for your first day, 'cause you don't know how we play. Maybe tomorrow or the next day, once I test you on the rules, you can join in."

Joyce never passed Martha's test, and as she seemed to take the lead, none of the other girls even bothered to test her; they simply ignored her completely. Did they have periods too? Had they "started" yet, Joyce wondered. Though some did have hints of a bust, they just seemed to be carefree and giggly.

In fact, the whole of the first week in her new school was spent in a daze for Joyce, who tried to hold herself together by concentrating on the new lessons and at recess time, finding a quiet corner to hide in while the minutes dragged by.

At least the bleeding had stopped. "Your period is over now Dear, for another month," her aunt had explained. Joyce still wasn't sure if she was supposed to feel better or worse for hearing that report. It all seemed such a messy business. Was her future under some curse?

Edmonton, Autumn 1938

Inside her new home, everything was very tidy and orderly. Teacups were pristine inside the china cabinet, clear of clutter, with only the occasional knickknack adorning a table. "I do like everything in its place, I must admit," Aunt Lou commented. "Then you know where to find things when you need them." Joyce found herself a little worried about being careless with where she left a book or a glass.

Back home, her mother was always prodding them to pick up after themselves. Sweaters were discarded over the arms of living room couches and chairs, books were scattered here and there, cards were fanned out on tables, games were unfinished—it was quite chaotic. A ball or running shoes were often left in the parlour, but no one seemed to notice, until their mother screeched at them to pick them up. Billy's toys were to be kept in their mother's room, but occasionally he would drop a toy car or building block in the hallway after carrying it with him for a teething object. No one ever owned up to having left anything out of place of course. When asked, "Who left their jacket out here?" there was always a quick chorus of "It wasn't me!"

Here, in Edmonton, the kitchen counter tops were free from cooking utensils and food items. There were no meat pies nor casseroles steaming on the countertop, nor half-eaten dinners, dirty spoons of Billy's cluttering things up, nor droplets of tea or milk staining the surfaces.

Here, the living room was smart and tidy, the furniture gleamed from regular polishing, tables were dust free and empty of boys' telltale articles. There also were no bowls of apples, no family knickknacks passed on from the cottage in

Muskoka, no cups and saucers for serving tea to her mother's music students. Her aunt's house was pristine and clutter-free. And quiet. Much quieter than home.

Meals here were much simpler as well. They had roast chicken or beef on Sundays, which Aunt Lorna served with boiled potatoes, vegetables and gravy, and used the leftovers the next day in a casserole. That was a bit like her mother did. But her aunt also made a few things Joyce had never had before, like creamed salmon, which tasted all right. Overall, the food was fine. Joyce liked Lorna's cooking fairly well. It was just the quiet at mealtimes she found hard to get used to. Billy was not there for her to coo over and look after. She missed hearing a new word he'd learned, praising him for it, or for a picture he'd drawn. Andrew was not there to ask questions about her homework, and she even found she missed being teased by Robert and David.

But then, Aunt Lorna gave her undivided attention. She answered all her questions without a fuss. She encouraged her in her schoolwork, always asked how she was feeling, and so far, never scolded her. That was something she didn't miss about being at home. Her mother was often shouting at her for things which really were not her fault. "Didn't you notice Billy dropping his car there—someone could trip and break their neck!" Joyce, can't you see the laundry needs to be taken upstairs?"

Aunt Lorna did ask Joyce to do some chores as well. It wasn't a holiday. She was expected to keep her room tidy, make her bed, and on weekends, they would do the dusting together, and Joyce would help with the dishes. But with just two of them, and no annoying brothers to mess things up the second you cleaned up, housework was a quick and simple task.

After dinner each evening, Lorna always offered to help Joyce with her homework, but most days she felt she could manage things on her own. She enjoyed staying in the living room while Aunt Lorna was reading or doing her own "homework." "You know, Dear, paying bills and so on ..." Although she missed her family desperately Joyce did like the feeling that her aunt was always there if she had any questions.

Sometimes the young niece would look up from her work and just check something with her aunt. She didn't want to trouble her too much, but it was really lovely to just be able to make sure she had understood her homework correctly. So strange really to have her aunt all to herself.

It was all just so very different here. The weather, of course, was much, much colder, though it was mostly a dry cold and Joyce didn't mind that. Aunt Lorna had kindly outfitted her with plenty of warm clothing and winter boots. In fact, when she thought about it, she was actually much warmer outdoors here than she had been back home in her thinner older overcoat and unlined boots. Anyway, she spent less time outdoors now that she took the bus to and from school. It was too far to walk, and Aunt Lorna was unable to ferry her back and forth due to her work schedule.

Each day, her aunt kept asking how she liked her new school. "Is your teacher paying enough attention to you? Are you making new friends? What games do you like to play with the other girls?"

Ever conditioned with good manners, Joyce answered as briefly as possible. "Yes, fine thank you," regarding the new school. As for new friendships, her standard answer was, "Slowly. It takes time."

Lorna knew those words were not her own. They were the kind of sentences her sister had surely pronounced in yet another of her talks before Joyce had left home. "Try not to complain, Dear. It will probably take a while to make new friends. Just try your best to fit in." Lorna sighed, as again she could imagine it all too well.

Alone at night in her bedroom, Joyce often opened her dresser drawer to find her treasures from home. She didn't always take them out to admire them. When she did display them, stroke them, gaze at them, it evoked a heavy melancholy in her. Instead, she decided just to check they were still waiting for her. The music medal, the perfume, Billy's toy bear... they all waited. Amidst the pristine new room, the revamped wardrobe and trappings of her new life in the west, they waited.

Across the hall, Lorna often lay awake brooding about her new charge, and whether she was doing her best to make her feel at home. She thought it certainly must feel strange and probably too quiet for Joyce compared to what she was used to. Although in the main, she felt "aunting" came very naturally to her. In fact, she found she surprised herself with how well she felt she was doing. She felt largely happy with the answers she gave to Joyce's questions. It didn't seem a struggle, and her niece even issued the odd smile and even a laugh from time to time. It was just ... well ... Lorna knew she could never replicate her home life; that was impossible. And she just couldn't help wishing her young niece could make new friends at school. She sensed the girl was holding back a lot. So many things unspoken ...

Once a week or so, Lorna reminded Joyce to write to her mother. "I will, Aunt Lou, but there isn't much to say since the last letter. And I've only received one letter from mother since I left home."'

"I know, and you must be missing her. And your brothers—even those two younger scamps." Always careful to avoid criticising Joyce's mother, Lorna added, "But remember, we have a bit more free time than your mother does, Dear. Why don't you write about some of the things you've learned at school, a tidbit or two of history. Have you ever written to her about Medicine Hat? I bet she's never heard of it! That would impress her!" Lorna winked in shared pride.

"Suzie No Mates"

After over a month in the new school, Joyce still didn't feel welcomed into the circles of girls who played together on the playground. Recess was the most torturous part of her day. As soon as the bell clanged for the fifteen-minute break, the class funnelled outdoors, and quickly clustered into bubbles of threes and fours. Boys would kick balls to one another, girls would skip rope or just lean against the building, buzzing with chatter. Teachers took it in turns to patrol the playground, and Joyce hoped she went unnoticed. She prayed they wouldn't pull her along to join the other girls. Standing in shaded corners, she kept her head bowed as the endless minutes dragged by.

Joyce began to dread her aunt pumping her for details about the other girls when she got home. Although Aunt Lou was kind and gave her plenty of attention, there were some things she'd rather not talk about yet. "What are some of your friends' names, dear? What games do you like to play together? Perhaps you'd like to invite one of them home here for lunch one Saturday?" The twelve-year-old newcomer always found a way to dodge these questions, giving fairly vague answers.

In truth, Joyce wasn't at all worried about making new friends. After all, she would be moving back home after two years anyway. It still seemed a long time away. Long, but not the forever feeling it had first seemed. She'd had her second period. Aunt Lorna worked out about when it would be due and circled it on the December page of the calendar. She quietly left on Joyce's bed plenty of supplies for what now was a monthly event.

Except the young adolescent really preferred to avoid looking at the calendar. There was nothing on it she wanted to see. It would be twenty-four months before she would see her family and friends again. And now each month was marked with a glaring "P" on one square. It made her feel exposed. Her femaleness seemed to be the cause of so many problems. Somehow, although she couldn't work out why, it seemed to be the reason she had been sent away from home. She felt a vague sense of shame. Just before lights out each night, she tensed her muscles, squinted and gulped as she forced herself to look at the calendar. It was now November 16. November 17 was circled with a large "P" beside it. It was the only handmade mark on any of the dates. Sure enough, it came the following day.

It still seemed to her that she was the only one she knew who menstruated.

Favourite Subjects

Rather than working to make new friends, Joyce concentrated on catching up with her schoolwork, which was a little different to what she was used to back in Ontario. Some of it was easy, and she had already covered it in earlier grades. Other things were more difficult, like science, but there was something new as well. They were all learning French, and Joyce absolutely adored it.

Back in Ontario, on her way home from school, she walked most days with Marg. But her friend lived closest to the school, so as Joyce continued along the last stretch to her own home alone, she often conjugated verbs in her head as she walked. Not to pass the time, she just ... loved ... words.

"I go, you go, he/she goes, we go, you go, they went." She hadn't noticed when speaking how funny English was. It was only by studying English that she observed so many contradictions. For example, the third person was singular yet the verb to match it was sometimes plural and vice versa. Things like that! "I play, you play, he plays! We play, you play, they play!" That was an example, or "I do, you do, he does, we do!" Singular noun, plural verb! People just seemed to know how to say things without being corrected, but when Joyce wrote it down, or read it, it was funny how the words were put together in strange ways.

Her grammar teacher called these things "irregular" verbs—it was where the verb didn't match up with the noun in a way. Or it didn't even match up with the "to" form, like the verb "to be," for example. It wasn't "I be, you be, he be," etc. Instead, it was "I am, you are, he/she is," then "we are, you are and they are." You'd never say, "I be, you be, he bes!"

A lot of the boys in her class hated grammar and said it was stupid. "It's useless. What difference does it make?" Yet Joyce thought it was fascinating, and to her it was very important. To speak, read and write properly, learn new words, and speak without making errors to her was a thing of beauty.

Joyce even practised spelling in her head. A word like "pneumatic" with a silent "p" was another exception in the English language. Words with "ough" were also interesting. The word was pronounced differently, depending on what the word was. "Thorough" was "a long 'o' sound," but "cough" had the same "ough" letters and was pronounced like "awff" instead. With spelling, her teacher had taught them some little sayings to help them remember, like "'I' before 'e' except after 'c,' or when it says 'eh' as in neighbour and sleigh. Another one was, "When two vowels go walking, the first one does the talking, like in "seat" and "aunt." With that thought, suddenly Joyce realised that the word "niece" was an exception to this rule. She was a niece. She was an exception, in both ways; the word and her as a person. She wasn't sure why, but this thought became a feeling which lasted for a few minutes and it was quite pleasant. Certainly Joyce really enjoyed everything to do with language. Her brain was porous for absorption of all things to do with speech, reading and writing.

Now, as she walked the fifteen minutes to the school bus, she did the same sort of head work but in French. "*Aller*—to go, *je vais, tu vas, il/elle va, nous allons, vous allez, ils/elles vont.*" And, "*etre*"! It was funny, because the verb "to be" in French was "*etre*" and like in English, conjugation of the infinitive or "to" form didn't look like the "to" form. *Etre* was conjugated as "*Je suis, tu es, il/elle est, nous sommes, vous êtes* (a little similar), *ils/elles sont.* Just like in English, the conjugation was totally different from the infinitive or "to" form, at least in the case of *etre* and *aller* ... and others too.

French was definitely a little harder though, because of the genders of all the nouns: everything was either masculine or feminine. Then the adjectives had to agree with the nouns too. For instance, *la table* ... now that one seemed to flow naturally. It seemed to make sense that it was feminine. But then if it was a beautiful table, it had to be "*une belle table*." It couldn't be a *beau* one! Also, that was an exception, because the adjective was *before* the noun, instead of after, as it usually was. These points were going to take a little longer to memorise, but still ... It was all quite a lot of fun.

Joyce stepped onto the bus and found a seat on her own. She had grown accustomed to sitting near the front so that she didn't have to walk past the other students to get off the bus, and she preferred to be fairly close to the driver. Suddenly she could hear stifled giggling behind her. She realised she'd gasped and uttered a French word or two aloud. She turned to see three girls two seats behind covering their mouths as they laughed. One mouthed "*Merci, Madame*" mockingly. As she quickly turned to face forward again, tears were stinging her eyes. Defiant, she held her head up.

When she got home that evening, she was determined not to tell Aunt Lorna what had happened on the bus. She was grown up enough to know to ignore the teases of the other girls, and she would learn not to let things upset her. It still stung though.

As they went into the house together, her aunt spotted a letter which had landed on the floor in the front hall. Look, Joyce, it's for you! Lifting the envelope, Joyce recognised her brother's writing and ran to her room to read it.

Dear Joyce (don't worry, you probably will never be called Jocie again!),

How are things in the Rockies? Have you climbed one yet? (Haha, just joking, it's a bit cold for that just yet). How do you and Aunt Lorna get along together? Have you settled in well, and how is your new school? I bet you are top of the class there, especially in English and spelling. Have you made any new friends yet? I saw Marg the other day. She says she really misses you. Well, we do too, just a bit. (Ok, joking again!) We all miss you, Joyce!

Life here is pretty much the same. I'm trying to study for my final exams next spring. Robert pretty much ignores his schoolwork but never misses a football practice. David is his irritating self as usual, and Billy is growing up a bit. He's almost saying Joyce properly now, so as I say, you might never get called Jocie again! He asked where you were a few times, so I told him you had gone to study the big mountains and you would come back and tell him lots of stories about it. He seemed happy with that!

Mother is busy as ever, teaching music, running the household and all of us. I'm sure she must find it hard being outnumbered by us fellows now, but you know Mother, carries on regardless.

I know you are busy, Joyce, but please try to find time to write me a few lines when you can. I would love to hear how you're getting along.

Yours sincerely,
Your brother Andrew

Andrew

Joyce clutched the letter to her chest and sighed heavily. The letter made her almost laugh, almost cry ... almost shout. But there seemed to be something missing from it as well. Nothing she could put into words. Just not the whole story somehow. "Oh, Andrew, so lovely to get your letter. You're wonderful." It was even nice to hear about ordinary life, like Robert going to football, and David annoying his brothers. As though not too much had changed. She felt a slight ache in her heart, but somehow it was ... all right. Everything at home was all right.

She decided she must organise her time so she could write back to Andrew within the next week or so. Then, remembering her Aunt Lorna, she grasped the pages and dashed into the living room, keen for her aunt to read her brother's letter.

Immersed in her newest library book, Lorna didn't look up at first. Then, realising, she shamefully shook herself back into the room. How old habits die hard. She had forgotten herself, forgotten her beloved niece. For a few greedy moments, she was back to her single life where her time was her own.

Quickly recovering herself, Lorna enthused over the letter from her nephew, which made receiving it all the richer for Joyce. Unlike her sister Isabelle, Lorna thought Andrew to be a great letter writer, including lots of questions for Joyce, plenty of encouragement and little tales of her other brothers and school happenings. Though respecting the young girl's privacy, she was delighted her niece was happy to share the letter with her.

Lorna suspected Andrew had written the same day Joyce left, rather than waiting to receive one from her as her mother had done. She must also write to Isabelle again soon to reassure her that Joyce was safe and well and settling in nicely. She wouldn't write "happy," not quite yet. She had written soon after Joyce arrived to let her sister know she had gotten there safely, but it was time she wrote again, even if Isabelle was poor at writing back.

Letters Home

Replying to Andrew's letter wasn't too hard at all. Joyce wanted him to think of her as grown up enough to handle things on her own and not to worry about her. She told him about her new home, her new school, about Aunt Lorna and the nice times they had together, that she had been to see the Rockies a few times, and how magnificent they were. She added that her aunt was teaching her how to cook and that Andrew should be happy that she had joined the library. "I might never be as smart as you, Andrew, but I'm sure going to give it a try." She was learning to be a little more lighthearted.

It was at recess one afternoon when suddenly, she had an idea. She could actually start communicating in French! Now she knew what she would do——she could write part of her letter home to her mother in French: *Bonjour, Maman, comment-allez vous? Je parle (j'ecris) en Français parce que j'ai commencé à apprendre un peu le Français. Quel temps fait-il là? Il fait très froid ici. Il neige beaucoup. Comment vont mes frères?*

Exceptionally, Joyce was absorbed in her own thoughts during the fifteen-minute break. She started "writing" a few lines in her head on the playground when Martha sneaked up behind her, making her jump.

"So ... why did you move to Edmonton then? Your Dad change his job?" her voice drawled slightly.

"No ... he—my father—moved away. My family's in Ontario. My mother ... so I came to live with my aunt."

"Ontario? Where's that, like the moon? Hahaha, that's why you talk funny. You don't sound like us. If you can't talk like we do, maybe you better go back where you came from."

"I can't—I can't go back—I—I'm here for two years—I," Joyce's throat tightened with fear and upset.

Martha bent to shove Joyce, but her arm was caught by a tall boy. "Ow, get offa me, ya redskin. You shouldn't be here neither. Get away." The boy loosened his grip on Martha, and she turned and ran off.

Joyce, grateful but a bit frightened of the boy as well, said, "Er ... thank you. I think you scared her away."

"She's afraid of anyone who is different. That's why she acts like that. I don't think she'll bother you anymore. If she does, I'm always around."

Joyce looked up into his calm face. He had a different smell ... like ... maturity. "What's your name, then?"

"Charlie. What's yours?"

Joyce told him her name in full, then added, "What's your second name?"

"Charlie."

"No, I meant your ... uh ... your family name?"

"Charlie. My name is Charlie Charlie."

Involuntarily, Joyce chuckled a little, then braver, said, "Charlie Charlie. Really?"

"Yes, a lot of us are called Charlie ... or Charles."

"In the same family?"

"In the same tribe. It makes it easier for white people to remember our names." His mouth widened into a sly smile.

Joyce was both fascinated and still a little frightened, but the young boy asked the next question. "You're new to the school too, aren't you." Charlie said it as a statement instead of a question.

"Yes, I just came a few weeks ago."

"We started here last September. Well, I did. My brother's in high school here. We live with a foster family in town. We are lucky that at least there are two of us, but you, you are on your own?"

"Yes, my brothers are back home in Toronto with my mother. I came to live with my aunt for two years because my mother couldn't afford to feed all of us anymore. Why did you come here?"

"I think the church thinks we are growing up like heathens and need to be educated properly. To get away from the old ways of our parents and grandparents ..."

"What is a heathen?" Joyce suddenly gave no further thought to shyness. She quickly started to feel more comfortable with Charlie.

"Our families are used to hunting and living off the land, always teaching children by showing them how to do things and drawing pictures for them about how to hunt, how to fish, how to carve, how to live. We draw a lot to learn instead of writing, you see. But the church believes this is against God, so they took us away from our families and brought us here to live in towns and cities and to stay with Christian families. We even had to learn English too."

Joyce never really thought about the church very often. It was simply a regular part of her life back home, like school and her family life. She just knew she saw most of her friends there, and her mother played the organ on Sundays while the choir sang. She found it quite nice really. Her brothers sometimes complained about going, but she had mostly enjoyed it.

Here, she and her Aunt Lorna went to church together most Sundays. The church was not quite the same as her Anglican church at home. Like many other churches in Edmonton, her aunt's Lutheran Church was a modern building. It had no organ, but still had a minister, and a choir.

She wasn't quite sure what to say next. "Where do you come from, Charlie?"

"Stoney Plain. It's a reservation."

Joyce didn't know what that meant either, but she was beginning to get a strange feeling being around Charlie. It wasn't unpleasant; it was quite nice in fact. But it seemed to be a sign that there were more changes coming.

The bell rang to signal the end of the break and Joyce and Charlie ran for the school entrance.

As the weeks progressed, Joyce found herself avoiding the girls and instead, looking for Charlie. He showed her a jumping game which involved hopping over a rope tied to his ankle. It wasn't quite the same as skipping rope, but it was more fun than trying to find something to do on her own. And whenever Charlie was around, she felt safe. He had been right: Martha and her friends now stayed well away.

Still, something told her she shouldn't mention Charlie to her aunt. She didn't really know why. It was just a feeling.

Charlie

Week after week, evenings in the foster home replicated each other, like copies of history books given to each pupil. Sitting quietly at the dinner table with his brother and foster family, Charlie bowed his head as grace was said. In fact, he kept his head down for most of the meal. He was unused to making too much eye contact. But this was another thing his foster parents complained about.

Dinnertime was the young Native's least favourite part of the day. He couldn't settle into the formality of the mealtime routines of this family. He felt ill at ease with these people who were family to one another and despite what they claimed, not his family. Although he had grown somewhat used to the meals of roast beef, potatoes, gravy and vegetables, he still missed the cornbread, wild rice and moose meat he had grown up on. As Joyce had pointed out, he was lucky to have his brother with him. But he sorely missed being with the rest of his family: his parents, uncles, aunts and cousins.

What was so wrong with it all anyway?

"Go on, Charlie, have some more potatoes." His foster mother tried to be kind, but he knew she would only be patient for so long and eventually he'd be sent to his room. Funnily enough, he preferred it there anyway. He'd never feel at home here. He could never completely fit in.

His foster brother, Neil, and foster sister Linda also tried to tease Charlie and his brother Reval into eating a little more. "C'mon, big brothers, if you don't eat more than that, we'll soon be bigger than you are." Their smaller, thinner selves laughed at the thought. His own brother Reval also had trouble eating a full meal of the more refined foods.

Charlie's foster mother especially, was always telling him he would feel better if he read the Bible more. She kept referring to different passages and had given him the New Testament to take up to his room. Charlie had tried, but he found that the more he tried to be Christian, the sadder he felt. During the autumn, his parents would be making the last preparations for winter. They would be asking the Great White Spirit for wisdom, and they would be waiting for signs, directing them in the final days of the hunt. How he longed to be there with them.

The two foster sons shared a room on the third floor of the house, which was something. At least they could spend some private time together, remembering their real parents and their lives back in Stoney Plain. His brother sometimes managed to find a scrap of wood and a small pen knife, and would sit quietly whittling, fashioning a bird or a beaver, clinging to the tiny hint of their early home life. He would often promise Charlie he would find a way back there for both of them.

Perhaps if they ate less and less and became ill enough they would send them back home to their mother and father, Charlie wondered. (Good idea, that was why Joyce was sent away ... because they couldn't afford to feed her.)

Charlie's new educational environment took some time to adjust to as well. But he was glad to have found a new friend. Joyce was quite quiet like he was, but shy. He wasn't timid, he was just ... quiet. To himself. She was the only one he knew who was newer to the school than he was, and just as unsettled. Being older, and having been there longer, he felt very compelled to encourage her and help her adjust to the new school. Finding Joyce made him feel so much more comfortable during his school day. They were from such different worlds yet seemed to share so much. He smiled thinking about how Joyce had told him she was always behind on her letter-writing to her family back home. That was a great difference between them: he and his brother were not allowed to write to their parents. Perhaps he could find some way …

Curiously, the young foster son also felt he should keep the fact of his friendship with Joyce quiet, even from Reval.

Toronto, Late November 1938

A few weeks after the new chaps had settled into their rooms, Isabelle left David, now turned eleven, in charge of watching Billy while she did a bit of grocery shopping. Robert, as usual, was at the football field, and Andrew had gone to the library. It was Saturday afternoon, a crisp clear day and Isabelle decided to go for a trail around the shops. Taking the bundle buggy to load her food purchases into, she set off with a light step. Exceptionally, she was feeling quite relaxed. She was looking forward to having a bit of time to herself, a rare moment without children to look after or meals to prepare.

As she browsed, she reflected on how life had settled down quite a lot since the two gentlemen had moved in. They both seemed pleasant enough, and thankfully, paid their rent on time. They even praised her meals! Compliments were something rarely heard in her house prior to their arrival! Breakfast time was a little chaotic, but she'd started to get organised by telling everyone they had to be seated around the table by seven thirty if they wanted anything to eat. She now just placed the porridge, bread and condiments on the table, and everyone helped themselves. It meant getting up very early and giving Billy his breakfast first, but that was fine.

Lunches were another matter, and a lot more work, but also resulted in a little more money coming in. She told the boarders and the older boys that if anyone wanted packed lunches, they were to tell her at the beginning of the week. She asked the boarders for an extra dollar per week for the midday meal, and she made it clear there were no food options; they got what they were given. Mr. Griffiths, with his nine-to-five job, was in more of a routine than Mick Sharp because of his shift work. And more work for her since his lunch needs were at odd hours. She realised she would have to remind Mick to give her notice if he wanted his lunch. All in all, everything had all come together quite nicely.

She would soon have to start preparing for Christmas! Aside from introducing some carols to her students, she would have to start thinking about the Christmas concert and services at church. She did enjoy the preparations for Christmas. It included some of her favourite pieces. When she practised the joyous Christmas music, everyone seemed more cheerful, especially the carols everyone loved. And this year, she had a new one, at least one she hadn't played before: "The Huron Carol '' by Saint Jean Brébeuf. It had recently been set to English words. "'Twas in the moon of wintertime when all the birds had fled that mighty Gitchy Manitou sent angel choirs instead." She hummed the haunting melody of half tones under her breath as she shopped.

Unbeknownst to the mother of five, a history book which sat upstairs in her eldest son's bedroom referred to Brébeuf and his torturous quest to convert Native peoples to Christianity, battling on foot through difficult Canadian terrain and opposing tribes. More ironic still, her daughter had herself forged a solitary journey through this same territory which gave birth to the priest's composition which Isabelle now played on the piano.

It didn't take long to nip around the A&P, as she only needed some flour, sugar, eggs and ... debating ... decided to buy a whole chicken for Sunday dinner; the leftovers were always great. She chuckled a little to herself, thinking of how the boys teased her over her meal stretching techniques. But now at least, her food budget went a little further.

She thought then of her husband, soon to be ex-husband, and realised it was the first time he had crossed her mind in ages. He sent the odd letter with a short message to the children, and included some money, but never sufficient to meet their needs. That was it. Her marriage was finished. It was unlikely he would even be seeing Andrew, his firstborn son and namesake again since he'd moved to Bancroft with his ... his ... new... hmm, individual ... whatever her name was.

But then ... perhaps all was for the best. She was quite enjoying her independence. Imagine it—she was now actually running a small business!

She decided to take a little look in Kresge's. When was the last time she had shopped there? She couldn't for the life of her recall. They had quite a good haberdashery department. Perhaps she could even find the money to take that weaving course advertised at the local college one evening a week. She'd always yearned to learn a new craft such as weaving.

Delighted to find several affordable spools of weaving cotton, she decided to take the step of purchasing them, as a tangible sign of her desire to become a weaver, and she would see if she could afford a loom next year.

Suddenly, Joyce and Lou came to mind. How little she had thought of them that whole afternoon! Chastising herself, she made a note to write on the calendar a time to write to each of them. Perhaps she could find a small present for both of them and send it on for Christmas, although it was cutting it a bit fine for time. Taking one last turn around the shop, she spotted some colourful hair combs. Had Joyce grown her hair a little longer now? Did Lou still wear hers in a French roll? Finding sufficient coins in her purse, she selected a pink one for Joyce and an ivory-coloured one for her sister. Clutching them to her breast for a sweet second, she then dashed to the checkout to pay for her purchases and stepped from the shop.

Her high spirits returning, she quickened her pace for the return home. Rushing up the steps and swinging open the door, she called, "Who can help little old me with my parcels?"

The house seemed eerily quiet. Had her older boys not returned yet? Where were the six male inhabitants of the house? Then, glancing into the parlour to her right, she saw Mr. Griffiths playing with Billy.

"And-Ro-David! Where are you? Come downstairs, please, now!"

Andrew

It was midweek, late evening, and the hum of the household was beginning to subside for the night. Upstairs in his bedroom, Andrew squinted through horn-rimmed glasses at his mathematics textbook. He had read and reread the same equation over and over, more than twenty times at least in the last fifteen minutes. "Harrumph," he shrugged.

Giving in to his own distractions, he swivelled off his chair, and walked over to open his door to check the old clock on the hall bookshelf. It was nearly ten o'clock. Mother would be calling up for lights out soon. Normally, he would have completed his homework in all subjects long before this time, so he could spend a bit of time with the family or his own reading choices.

Where was the "brainbox" as his friends at school had called him? Since his father had left, his mother started calling him "the man of the house." Really?

The movements he had made since coming home from school filed through his head.

Before peeling the potatoes for dinner, he had worked in the parlour. Dust particles had filled his nostrils as he brushed past the velvet curtains which gated the high ceilings and crimson chesterfield. He had swept the floor, dusted his mother's sideboard and dining table, grazed over the china cabinet, but polished to a high gloss her piano and bench. The instrument was what earned the family a few extra coins per week, so he needed to take good care of it. Aside from her piano students, his mother spent several hours per day practising her music for Sunday service, so it was the most important piece of furniture in the room. It "earned" its keep and warranted extra care.

Working from the base end of the piano, Andrew had cleaned key by key, white then black, white then black, each emitting a sour sound in the monotone ritual. As the notes had reached the higher tones, his thoughts shifted from mother to his sister. How long had she been away now—six weeks—and he had no letter from her yet. He presumed she had already received at least the first if not the second of his.

He hoped it was a good sign that she was busy with her new school and hopefully she and Aunt Lorna were getting on well together. Perhaps Joyce hadn't really had time to write— or was she staying quiet because she didn't want to worry him? Besides, he and his mother and brothers only had one person to write to. Joyce had potentially five of them to correspond with ... not counting Billy of course. But Mother had had two letters already; she had read them aloud at the dinner table. Both had reported everything was going well, everything was fine. "Aunt Lorna is very nice and so is my school. It is very new with lots of new books, and I'm studying hard ..."

He didn't really trust his sister's words to his mother. The eldest son was certain Joyce would write more openly and frankly in a personal letter to him.

If he was honest, which of course he hadn't been ... his younger sister seemed too young and small to be going off across the country all on her own. Sighing, he imagined her curling up against the cold train window as it snaked and dragged her across the prairies. He wished he could have kept her at home. He wished he could have protected her from this punishing journey, a two-year sentence—a lifetime surely to her—away from home to stay with her elderly maiden aunt. He'd tried valiantly with his mother to make the case for keeping Joyce at home, but as with most things, his mother's decision had been made. But then, it wasn't really his mother's fault. If only his father hadn't had to leave. He had left them in such a mess, the bounder. Andrew didn't care if he never saw him again. His mother never even mentioned his name anymore. His clothes and belongings had quickly been banished from the house. It was as though he had been gone for many years or died. But he knew his father's departure had been difficult for all of them, and Andrew knew instinctively that it was hardest on Joyce.

"Why is Mother sending me away? What have I done?" Joyce's sweet face interrogated his own. Soon that sweetness would dissipate, swallowed by womanly knowing. He had seen his little sister for the last time. Not Joyce, he would see her again, but she would no longer be his little sister.

"She's not. You're not being sent away. And you've done nothing wrong, Joyce. You mustn't think that. Didn't Mother explain that money is short now that Dad has gone away, and Aunt Lorna has offered to have one of us help out for a while. You'll be getting to travel all the way across the country, Joyce. You're lucky, really. You'll be the first one of us to see the Rockies. You'll love it, you'll see. We all wish we could go!"

"But I don't want to leave home. Why does it have to be me? David would love to go. He told everyone he would. I don't want to be away from home, away from you. I don't eat that much. I can eat less. Tell her, please, Andrew. She won't even know I'm here. And I will work harder at home. Just please ask her not to send me away."

"I've tried, Joyce, but it's hard for her these days, you know. But really, you should just think what a great adventure you'll be having, while the rest of us are stuck at home doing the same old things." Andrew's tone was straining to sound encouraging.

"But that's just it. Why do things have to be different? Why did Father have to go away?"

His mother did sometimes seem to have a way of driving people away. Robert spent most of his time either playing football or practising for a game. He often managed to avoid chores this way as well, usually arriving after most of the work had been done. But then, Mother mentioned briefly that Robert might get to university on a scholarship as well. Then he would be gone for good also. That was an easy escape for Robert, and a pipe dream for Andrew. There simply would never be the money available for a university education for him. It was a shame in a way that he was academically inclined rather than athletic, like Robert.

Joyce's absence from their lives seemed to leave the biggest void for Andrew. Billy was too little to notice much when things changed. David, at eleven, was already sweeping out the coalbin and making beds, which was something. Although Joyce was right, David could be a little so and so at times ... already becoming a real know-it-all.

Things had been so different when his father was around. There was more laughter in the house in the evenings. Now everyone seemed to eat in silence, their mother taking their father's seat at the table and Andrew sitting in hers. Man of the house indeed. Everyone knew their place now.

The two boarders were all right. He did like Michael; he was full of life. And of course because Michael worked shifts with the police, he wasn't always around. Once in a while, the man brought his two boys over to play, which brought more life into the house. Paul was about five, a little older than Billy, and Leon was seven. They were nice kids, and Andrew felt a bit sorry for them as their parents were getting divorced. Just like his own. But at least Michael spent time with his children.

Mr. Griffiths was certainly polite ... but ... for some reason, Andrew couldn't relax around him. Mother liked him of course, because he always told her what a lovely meal she had made. He chuckled inwardly: at least the menus had improved since the boarders had moved in. Mother could now afford to buy more meat!

Andrew considered that it was two hours earlier in Alberta than in Ontario. He wondered whether Joyce had eaten dinner yet and if so, did she like Aunt Lou's cooking? He remembered Aunt Lorna a little bit from meeting her when he was about nine or ten. She seemed nice enough, perhaps a bit formal ... and very thin. He hoped his little sister was getting enough to eat out west! God, he did sound to himself more and more like a woman than a man of the house! Maybe this life of housework served him right! But the main point was, he hoped Aunt Lorna was kind. Joyce was already such a serious girl. She didn't need much correcting or improving.

"Andrew!" the certain call of his mother's voice drifted up the stairs, rousing him from his reverie. "It's after ten! Time for lights out. Can you make sure Robert turns his light out as well? Good night."

Edmonton, Late November 1938

Lorna was pleased to read in her sister's latest letter from Toronto that she now had two boarders ensconced at home. They had apparently settled in well with her boys, and the extra income had certainly helped stretch the family budget.

She knew her sister had suffered tremendously since her scoundrel husband had left and had felt completely ostracized by some of the neighbours. Divorce was still a big taboo in Ontario. Now with two new men under her sister's roof, she hoped the atmosphere in the neighbourhood hadn't got worse.

Lorna had become more relaxed about her role as guardian for Joyce. As the months passed, she was much less worried about all the details, and decided just to enjoy her niece's company. One unusually slow afternoon at work, Lorna suddenly realised she'd not even thought of Richard for weeks. She had answered Joyce truthfully when she'd asked her aunt about marriage.

From her perspective, she and Joyce had easily settled into a nice routine. Alternate Saturdays were spent at the library, once Lorna had ensured that Joyce did indeed like reading. She certainly didn't want to force things. Sometimes they would go to a movie together if there were any good ones for Joyce's age group, even a concert or two. They went to church most Sundays, and Lorna found they both seemed to enjoy singing hymns together. Afterward, they wondered together which hymns Isabelle would be playing in church back in Toronto.

Lorna liked to involve her niece in the grocery shopping as well, teaching her how to think ahead about the meals they would like to have during the week, and to make a list, to make sure she had all the ingredients. The young adolescent was very easy to please, good about eating vegetables, and anything put in front of her. Enticing her into the kitchen on occasion, Lorna had taught her how to make pastry and one or two new dishes.

After school, Joyce went to the Taylors, two doors down for an hour or two, until Lou got home from work. Joyce seemed to like going there and the childless couple in their sixties were delighted to have Joyce. Clare and Doug always prepared a snack for her when she arrived and passed the time playing cards or singing a song or two around the piano before Lorna collected her.

When Lorna had mentioned to the Taylors about Joyce's piano lessons back home, Alana suggested that Joyce could use their piano to practise on and find a local teacher. Thanking them, Lorna decided on reflection that Joyce could do with a break and would see first how much interest Joyce showed in carrying on with the instrument before organising lessons. With the move to the other side of Canada, getting to know her aunt, major physical changes, a new school ... piano lessons could take a back seat for a while.

In fact, rather than classical, Mrs. Taylor played more popular music, pieces such as "Oh Susanna," "My Bonnie Lies Over the Ocean," sing-a-long tunes which were a welcome holiday for Joyce after the classical works she was used to at home. "The old ones can be a bit heavy sometimes," Joyce remarked, and the Taylors chuckled.

In terms of Lorna's own life, work continued much as it had done, and with Joyce to think about, she was content enough. Since her niece's arrival, she had shelved any thoughts she'd had of seeking promotion, and she had no regrets. Rather than going out with Rhonda for an evening, her friend had come over to dinner once or twice, had been delighted to meet Joyce, and they had enjoyed a few laughs together, as Joyce said it was nice to be with "just the girls" for a change. Sometimes Lorna had met up with Rhonda at lunchtime for a private chat, and it was great to know her old friend was always there as a confidante. She had worried that Joyce had been a bit traumatised by the train journey and sudden arrival of her period, but Rhonda, as a mother herself, had reassured her how resilient young people are.

Joyce still didn't seem to have made any friends at school, or none that she spoke of. Curiously, Lorna felt that her niece didn't seem to mind either. Perhaps again, she had enough to cope with. Pre-teenagers could sometimes be a bit taunting, Lorna knew. Perhaps they had teased her because she was new and shy, and Joyce had withdrawn a bit.

She hoped Joyce would feel free to speak to her if she had any problems.

Western Winter

Winters in the West were considerably more severe than the mild climate in Toronto, but Joyce soon got used to wrapping up warmly whenever she went out and actually enjoyed crunching through the snow's crust as she walked with her aunt on a weekend jaunt. The air was always fresh with flurries or their promise.

Joyce's first Christmas in the west had been celebrated quietly at home with her aunt, who had taken a bit of extra time off to spend with her while she was on school holidays.

On a clear, mild day, they had wrapped themselves up, slid their feet into winter boots and driven to the Rockies. Dwarfed by the towering peaks which presided over the foothills below, they parked and took a hike on a lowly slope. Grabbing hold of each other's hands, they enjoyed the challenge of the rough terrain under their foot fall without the need to overdo it. Once or twice they were overtaken by a few more serious hikers, but were happy striding at their own pace. They didn't speak too often of the family back in Toronto, but as they walked, the subject opened naturally. "I wonder what Christmas music your mother will be playing this year?"

"I don't know, but it was always nice to hear her playing carols for the Christmas service, and sometimes we even used to sing together, like 'O Little Town of Bethlehem' and 'O Come All Ye Faithful.' That was lovely."

Lorna was pleased to hear Joyce reminiscing a little. The youngster's voice sounded level and calm.

Above them the snowy peaks were alive with skiers skimming through the December air. She caught herself dreamily thinking of Richard for a few absent moments, but quickly recovered herself. She had never mentioned him to Joyce of course. As Lorna herself didn't ski, she was somewhat in awe of the sport. "When you're older you might decide to take it up, Joyce. You might find some of your friends like to ski. It's for the braver heart than your old aunt!"

Her young niece reflected quietly for a few minutes, then took her aunt by surprise. "Did you never want to get married, Aunt Lou?"

Pausing as well before speaking, the aging woman responded diplomatically, "There was someone once, but it was a very long time ago, and it didn't work out. But I have no regrets, Joyce. I'm so happy that you have come to stay with me for a while. I'm so glad I stayed single, really, Dear. And what about you, Joyce? Would you like to get married when you're older?"

"No, I don't think so. No, I think I would like to stay single like you, Aunt Lorna, and have a career. Men just seem to upset things. My father went away and that upset everything."

"I know that has been really difficult, Joyce. I can understand your feelings, but someday ... you may change your mind."

Joyce could feel tears stinging in her eyes and was pleased the conversation was over, even though she had initiated it.

Christmas day was spent first attending church together, then exchanging a few presents.

Joyce had managed to make a small tote bag in home economics, on which she had hand embroidered "Lorna" and included a handmade bracelet of small pink and white crystal beads strung onto an elastic band. She was very proud of the whole gift and couldn't wait to see her aunt open it.

For Joyce, Lorna had framed an old family photograph she had found of herself with her brothers and sisters, including Isabelle of course, which she hoped Joyce would enjoy, and a new hat and mittens which she'd knitted herself.

Surprising Joyce on Christmas morning was another package, the sender of which Joyce had no idea. About ten days earlier, Lorna was astounded to receive a letter from Isabelle, with a little money for Christmas for Joyce. The short letter thanked Lorna for everything she was doing for the family and asked if she could please buy Joyce a small gift from all of them. It included the ivory and pink hair combs, and Lorna found herself thawing toward her younger sister at the touching gesture. She tucked it all away, feeling a thrill of anticipation.

During one of her lunch hours, Lorna managed to find a necklace and matching ring made from locally mined jewels. That could be from her mother and Andrew. Then finding a scarf which matched the hat and mittens she had made, she marked that from Robert, and wanting something more playful, she found a small rubber handball. Those could be from David and Billy. Goodness, the Christmas gifts made for quite a well-rounded celebration, she thought.

"Oh! Oh! Aunt Lou!" Joyce was almost speechless on opening all her gifts. As her aunt gave an encouraging nod, Joyce began to don the necklace, ring, hat, scarf, and mitts, and eyeing the little ball with glee, she scooped them up, and popped them into Aunt Lou's tote bag.

The ball, something Joyce never got around to playing with, was ultimately given to the next generation. Her daughter, Alana, born fourteen years later, made it a summer companion as she learned to play "Ordinary Movings."

"Perfect," said Lorna concurring. "You and I will have to have a game together after dinner—which I can smell calling us now!" Grabbing her niece by the hand, they bustled into the kitchen to put the finishing touches on their Christmas meal. Sometimes, Joyce admitted silently, it was lovely ... just the two of them!

Joyce didn't mind being away from home so much when she was spending time with her aunt. She loved reading together, learning to cook, listening to Aunt Lou's stories and even doing chores. It was her school life where she felt like a fish out of water. The academics were fine, it was just the other students.

When Lorna reluctantly returned to work after Christmas, Joyce stayed with their neighbours, the Taylors. She thought happily of new games she could play with the older couple and knuckled down to write an essay on how her Christmas holidays were spent.

Lou was grateful to her neighbours for looking after Joyce. Especially as she didn't feel comfortable leaving her all alone at home. But sometimes she did worry about Mr. Taylor. Since he'd retired, he did seem quite restless. He of course doted on Joyce, and Lorna had no qualms about that. But then of course she was a little girl, and naturally spent more time with Mrs. Taylor. Lorna had noticed when she picked Joyce up that she could sometimes smell alcohol on his breath.

Kindred Spirits

As Joyce returned to school in January after Christmas, her playtime breaks continued to be taken up with Charlie. He had taken to calling her "Eastern Princess" and as she gradually improved her skills on the rope jumping game, she noticed that Charlie grew more and more quieter. Initially she felt anxious about this and tried to engage with him by chatting more, but Charlie didn't respond much. More and more their time spent together was in companionable silence. She then remembered what he had first told her about how Indian people were used to learning by watching their parents and elders demonstrating how to do things, or by drawing pictures. Maybe Charlie grew more silent now that Joyce understood the game and could play it herself. She was learning so many things here outside the classroom.

Still, she decided one day to ask Charlie a little more about his feelings about living with ... foster parents, he called them.

"It's ok. We're sort of used to moving around anyway."

"Really, where else have you lived?"

"Well, our chief is a very smart guy. He cares a lot about all of us in the tribe. He wanted to work out all the trouble we were having ... so he moved all of us to another place, farther away from the cities."

"Why is that?" Joyce felt fright thickening just beneath her thin layer of bravery.

"Many years ago, we in the tribe were given alcohol by white people. It doesn't help us in the tribe, you see. It makes us crazy. Once we start drinking, we can't stop. Men become drunk a lot of the time. Then they cannot hunt and fish—they for sure cannot work in the factories white people have built. So our chief moved us far away from the bars and shops in the cities so we cannot buy alcohol anymore ..."

Listening attentively, Joyce gasped a little.

"To help us think differently, and be different, the chief even changed his name!"

"Really, what to ... err ... from what to what?"

"He used to be Chief White Cloud. Now he's Chief Wasacase."

"Chief Wasacase?"

"Yes, the chief used to drink a lot too, you see."

"Really?"

"Yes, but since the tribe went 'dry' he changed it to Wasacase. Because he 'WASACASE' like a case of beer, before when he was drinking ... but not anymore. It's in the past now. He *was* a case of beer—but he is no longer a case of beer! A warm smile spread across his face.

Charlie didn't speak a lot but when he did it was either very important or quite funny. Joyce had never seen her father or anyone else's father drink, at least not that she could think of. But she suddenly remembered the businessmen she had seen drinking on the train, how they had jeered at her, and how she had felt nervous being around them. She felt glad the chief had moved his people away from alcohol. It sounded like a good idea at least.

Charlie continued, "But like I told you before, the white men still think that we are not living properly. They don't believe in the Great White Spirit guides we believe in, and even though our villages became happy and peaceful again, the white people had to come in and take us away from our parents to live the way they live.... But I don't think we can ever be like white people. This is what white people will never understand. We live off the land; it is a part of us. Our life is hunting, fishing, using every part of what we shoot or catch for food, clothing and shelter. We make our own houses, our own tools, everything. We do not like man made things. We belong to the land. That is the only way we can survive."

It was the most, the longest, Joyce had ever heard Charlie speak. Now she was the silent one for some time. It was a lot to take in. Sadness and worry swirled inside her. "What will you do then, Charlie? Will you run away, back home to your parents?"

The question was left suspended in the air like a classroom question that couldn't be answered. The bell ended the conversation with a shrill note, calling them back into the school building.

That evening in her new home, Joyce felt rather more grateful than she had been for her warm surroundings and her doting aunt. Lorna still probed her about her friendships at school, until the tweleve-year-old finally explained to her aunt that the other girls had already made their own friends at the beginning of the school year, and that they were happy that way.

"Don't worry, Aunt Lou. I'm happy as I am too, really. It's important that I do well at school because you are so kind to have me here. I am happy to concentrate on my schoolwork. There will be plenty of time in the future to make friends."

"All right, Dear. Oh, before I forget, please can you check the mailbox? I wouldn't be surprised if there's some post for you." Lorna smiled at her young niece, of whom she was growing extremely fond, and wondered a little who was teaching whom about life!

Missing

As January slid into February, Joyce was on her own again at school. She hadn't seen Charlie there for a few days. His absence was unsettling, and she hoped he wasn't ill. She wished she had some way of getting some news of her friend.

Back home, if her friend Margaret had taken ill, her older sister would have told Joyce, or Joyce would have stopped by her house to check on her. Here, she didn't even know where Charlie lived and even if she did, she wouldn't have gone to the house. They wouldn't even know who she was. His older brother went to the high school, which was about a mile away from her school, so she had no way of checking with him.

After about four days, Charlie returned to school and on seeing him on the playground, relief flooded into Joyce's chest. Standing on his own, towering above most of the others, his head was down, and he scuffed one shoe on the courtyard.

Running up to him, she called out his name. "Where have you been? Have you been sick? I've missed seeing you, Charlie. I'm so glad you're back."

Slow to reply, Charlie finally said, "I may be sent away. My brother has been in trouble."

"Wh-why?" Shyness had found Joyce again.

"I better not say, Joyce."

"But … why?"

"I can't say, Joyce. Look, I don't know what's going to happen. Perhaps you should stay away from me for a while …"

Concentrating fully on Charlie, Joyce didn't notice two older girls charging around the school corner. Without warning, Charlie was assailed with a tirade of pushing and kicking launched by the girls. Joyce tried to intervene, but the bigger girls started pulling her hair and insulting her.

"You're an Indian lover. Get out of here. Get away, Indian lover!"

She pushed them back, instinctively. "You get away. Leave him alone!"

Joyce ran inside the school to find a teacher, but the corridors were empty. Then, breathlessly running into her classroom to find her teacher, she called, "Mrs. Waters, please come quickly. There's a fight on the playground!"

Her teacher then raced out behind Joyce and followed her to the scene. There was no sign of the girls, nor of Charlie. Her teacher shook her head and, pressing on Joyce's back, escorted her back into the classroom. The bell sounded the end of recess time then.

Joyce spent the rest of the school day feeling distressed and worried. Finally, she decided she must report the incident to her aunt when she got home.

Having difficulty eating her supper that evening, Joyce finally said, "Aunt Lou, I DO have a school friend, actually, but ..."

Aunt Lou listened sympathetically to the story and wondered aloud whether the schools were dealing with the bullying problem.

"But can't YOU do something, Aunt Lou?" Joyce implored.

The older woman struggled to answer her niece, who showed no sign of physical injury. However, her promise to herself that she would do everything possible to "understand, support, and generally look after Joyce to the best of her ability for two years" resounded in her ears.

"I'll go and speak to the school, Joyce. It is a terrible situation. I'm not sure how much I can do, because I am just your aunt, and you were mainly an observer of the occurrence, not a participant or a victim."

"But—"

"I know, I'm so sorry that this happened to Charlie and to you. I cannot go tomorrow as I will have to let work know, but I will go the day after—Friday."

After saying good night to her niece that evening, Lorna couldn't concentrate on her book. She hoped she hadn't sounded too dismissive of the incident to Joyce. She felt very protective of her, but also didn't want her young charge to take too many worries on her young shoulders.

"Those damn ne'er do wells!" she thought. She had read in the newspaper occasional accounts of indigenous children being taken from their homes, brought into residential care to be educated, and admittedly hadn't given it much further thought. She had not much contact with Native peoples.

Mainly her experience only involved driving by their communities. Once, however, when served by a young Indian waiter, she noticed the quiet gentleness he exuded. There was almost a sense of greater wisdom about him that Lorna had remembered. Perhaps she should make the effort to read more about the history of Native peoples and inform herself about their present life challenges.

When Lou visited the school, she was told, as she somehow expected, that there was little that could be done and in fact, the two brothers were likely to either be sent back to the reservation or more probably to reform school.

"The branch doesn't fall far from the tree, remember," the principal declared. "The younger brother will just take the example from the older one and he will soon start getting drunk as well. They're best in a penal institution."

"But they have been brought here from home by the local churches to be educated. Surely they can offer some support to these boys. Perhaps they are just not yet properly settled into their foster home ..."

"Now, how is Joyce getting on with her mathematics? It seems to be her weakest class." The principal changed the subject so abruptly that Lorna was completely dumbstruck.

"Mathematics?" That was one of her niece's best subjects! Lorna was incensed. Rising from her seat, she fixed the principal with a glare. "This school has a responsibility, not only to educate everyone in this school, but to ensure they feel safe here. If the children don't feel safe and secure, they can't learn!" With that, she informed him she had to get back home to her niece and hurried out of the building.

Lou was stymied as to how to report back to Joyce. The school head clearly didn't know the first thing about her niece and had not taken the time to investigate the issue at hand. And what future was there for a Native Canadian who effectively was yanked by the ear out of his home, and along with his brother, away from their parents without even hope of seeing them again?

After about ten days, Charlie returned to school, but Joyce was forbidden from seeing him on the playground. Mrs. Waters was adamant. "You shouldn't be playing with boys anyway, Joyce. And certainly not Indian boys! And he's older than you too! What's the matter with you, anyway? Go and play with the girls. Where's Martha and your other friends?"

"What other friends?" she reflected mutely. "I have no girlfriends. Martha certainly doesn't want to be with me. I'm used to being with boys. I have four brothers." But her teacher had been very clear with her, and the twelve-year-old was far too timid to even consider disobeying.

Charlie

Charlie's brother had started stealing small fifths of alcohol from a neighbour. They liked a drink and were out all day running a local general store. They always left their doors open and Reval started to sneak in after school "just for a nip. They won't miss it."

Charlie felt strange about his brother's theft. Even stranger when the amounts he took increased, he started offering it to Charlie before bed. "Only a little bit," his brother cajoled. "It will help you to sleep. A little won't hurt. White people look down on us and tell us not to do things that they do themselves, like drinking. They do it all the time. I'm tired of this. We just need to relax and wait to grow up a little more so we can leave this place behind for good."

The thirteen-year-old boy felt completely confused. He didn't know where to look for guidance. He'd always looked up to Reval, but now ...? His foster parents' house didn't feel like home—he couldn't really settle into their rules. He felt resented by his foster brother and sister. School was no better. Neither the teachers nor the other pupils accepted him. The teachers criticized him continually and tried to get him to change the way he spoke. Worse, he had no real friends. Well, except Joyce, but she was a young girl.

At first, he argued with his brother, reminding him of their chief and how against alcohol he was. He warned him about the trouble they could get into. But Reval made no response, except to tip the bottle down his throat.

Gradually, reluctantly, Charlie gave in to his brother and started taking a sip or two of the sour liquid. He winced and swallowed; its bitterness sliding into his stomach. He didn't want any more.

But next, the sinister fluid then made its way to Reval's school grounds. The teenager was caught drinking at school. His foster parents were called. He was given a severe warning and suspended from school for one week. With a promise to behave, the school authorities and his foster parents declared the matter brought to a close.

As his punishment of being banned from school was declared, Reval tried to stifle his grin over consequences which for him were more of a reward. He was relieved to be away from school, happy to be confined to his room, preferring to be alone.

Edmonton—Back at School

Having been warned off spending time together on the playground, Joyce passed the time during her breaks playing jacks on her own or the solitary jump rope game Charlie had taught her. Martha and her gaggle of girls stayed well away and that suited the newcomer just fine.

Occasionally she and Charlie nodded at one another across the playground, with Joyce chancing a brief smile once or twice and Charlie quickly averting his eyes.

The isolation continued for some weeks until one Thursday after school, as Joyce boarded the school bus, she sensed a long shadow behind her. Charlie!

He dashed onto the bus and slipped into the seat behind her.

"What are you doing, Charlie?" Joyce was nervous.

"I want to see where you live. It sounds nice."

"Wha—? But I'm going to stay with the Taylors now until my aunt gets home."

Charlie followed Joyce off the bus, and a stilted conversation ensued. "But," Joyce stammered, "Mr. and Mrs. Taylor don't know you. I think I should let them know—"

"You always made me feel like an equal on the playground, Joyce. But I guess when it really counts, I'm not welcome."

"No—it's not that—give me a chance to—I need to talk to my aunt first..."

Charlie stomped off as Joyce neared her neighbour's home. But after she was safely inside, he hovered nearby watching.

Doug Taylor later noticed the level in his whiskey bottle had dropped. While the couple entertained Joyce in the living room, Charlie had slipped into the kitchen area to search for alcohol.

After about a week of quarrelling between Doug and Clare, about how much Doug had been drinking, and not remembering how much he had drunk, the couple finally agreed something was amiss.

During the weekend when everyone was at home, they approached Lorna and questions were asked of Joyce. The twelve-year-old, puzzled, and a little frightened, denied any knowledge of any involvement. Lorna then supported her niece in her responses, telling her neighbours she was sorry about the alleged incident, but there was nothing more to be said about it for the moment.

After the Taylors went home, Joyce went to her room. She wanted to be on her own.

Lorna left her to reflect for a while. She was in no way suspicious of her niece, but the reported theft of her after school caregivers was certainly curious. She gathered herself together and knocked on Joyce's door. All was quiet for a while, then a soft voice said, "Come in."

Joyce was lying on the bed, facing toward the door. Lorna sat on the edge of the bed, resting her thin hand a few inches from Joyce. There was no eye contact.

"I'm worried that Charlie must have stolen that alcohol, Aunt Lou."

There was a pause. "But how does he know the Taylors?"

"He followed me there after school one day. He wanted to come in, but I told him I would have to speak to you first. He was upset, saying he wasn't welcome in my life. That's just not true, but I wanted him to be invited first, not just come unexpectedly. Oh, I feel so sad, Aunt Lou. He doesn't understand ..."

"I see. Yes, they may have different customs to us. We are used to being invited to places rather than just turning up. Both ways are fine, it's just ... the communication between people which is done differently."

"I don't want to get Charlie into trouble ..."

"I understand that, Dear. And we don't actually know if Charlie was the culprit in this case."

"No, we don't. He's innocent until proven guilty, isn't that right?"

Lorna stroked Joyce's hand and told her young niece not to worry anymore about the situation. "You've done nothing wrong, Joyce. You're not to let this bother you anymore. But if Charlie ever follows you after school again, you must tell me immediately, do you understand? But for now, leave it with me and I will have a think about what to do next. You relax here for a while, and when you're ready, come down and we'll have a cup of tea together."

Lorna decided to have a chat with Clare Taylor on her own. She explained what had happened, and gently shared Joyce's uneasy suspicions about Charlie. As Lorna expected, Clare was upset about the accusation of theft, which had mainly come from Doug. "He's convinced that he wasn't the one who had drunk all the whiskey, Lorna. He says there is definitely much less in the bottle than before. Oh, Lou, what are we to do? He actually wants to go to the police. As far as

I'm concerned, if there's less alcohol for him to drink, that can only be a good thing ... but ..."

"Okay, Clare, try not to worry about it anymore. Sometimes these things can be little blessings of learning for us all. Perhaps if we let things be for a little while, it all may quiet down in a week or so. But I've been thinking anyway that Joyce is going to be thirteen in a few weeks. She will be all right on her own for an hour or so now until I get home."

"Ah, please don't stop Joyce coming, Lorna. She is such a ray of sunshine in my day. In both of our days. You know Doug is not accusing Joyce of anything. He loves her to bits. We would both be so sad if we didn't get to see her."

"All right. We will continue as normal for the next couple of weeks and see how things go, but I will ask Joyce to promise to let me know immediately if Charlie ever follows her again."

Quiet was an understatement to the deafening silence which ensued in Joyce's friendship scene. The disappearing whiskey had been due to Charlie's actions. He and Reval had hatched a plan to get themselves kicked out of care and expelled from school to boot. Caught a short while later on a street corner near their foster home, the brothers were well on their way to a drunken stupor. Clutching pop bottles concealing cocktails of alcohol and cola, they were charged with underaged drinking and sent to reform school. As they had imagined, it didn't take much for the system to crash down on them and, revelling in its superiority, eliminate the boys from the mainstream.

Joyce learned of this from Martha, who enjoyed relating the whole report much too much. From then on, Joyce lost all interest in forging new friendships at school, retreating into her studies and clinging to her weekend cocoon at home with her aunt.

Worried that the incident had upset Joyce's school life, Lorna tried unsuccessfully to get her niece to plan a party for her thirteenth birthday in mid-February. Joyce insisted that she was happy to just celebrate at home, just the two of them, "Like we did at Christmas." In the end, Lorna convinced her niece that it would be fun to invite Rhonda and her family. Rhonda's son, though a couple of years older than Joyce, would balance things a little. It wasn't healthy for a girl of Joyce's age to be with adults all the time. Unfortunately, Joyce was not destined to forge friendships with her own age group for the duration of her two-year hiatus in the west.

Whether at home or school, isolation was a now lingering companion. Soon after her birthday, Lorna agreed that she could stay on her own after school, provided she locked the door and stayed inside until her aunt got home. Joyce was quite accepting of her time alone, sometimes even beginning the preparation for the evening meal.

Lost Friendship

Joyce became very subdued after the loss of Charlie's friendship. She continued to study hard and as ever, remained relatively quiet and reserved with her aunt. Lorna worried that Joyce was in fact too quiet, and tried reassuring, prompting, and even teasing her, but Joyce insisted that she was fine. "I want to work hard at school to make you proud of me, Aunt Lou. I want to become a Registered Nurse when I get older. Unless I join the circus!"

"The circus?" Aunt Lorna was incredulous. "What do you mean, Joyce?"

Joyce had never told her aunt about meeting Betsy on the train. Although such a vivid character, the time spent with her had been torpedoed by the onset of her menstrual cycle and settling into life in Edmonton. She then told her aunt about the circus entertainers and how much fun they were.

"But don't worry, Aunt Lou. I'm not really thinking of joining the circus. I'm too studious for that! I really and truly do want to be a nurse when I grow up."

Relieved but silent, Lorna put her arm around her niece. Her shoulder felt nearly as bony as her own. She closed her eyes and tilted her head to touch Joyce's. Secretly, the idea of returning to Ontario wasn't just for herself. She had grown so close to Joyce, she wished she could continue to protect her when she went back home.

Joyce clung to her for a few minutes.

Turning the Page

Charlie did not spend long in reform school. The two years passed quite quickly for him, as he developed an interest in drawing. He was later destined to join a group of Native artists, immersing himself in iconic Native art works as part of the Ducharme community of carvers, sculptors and painters.

Reval, similarly, continued to carve and sculpt. Drawing from his experiences both outside and inside the reserve, and coupled with his natural leadership instincts, Reval overcame his early challenges and became an elder of the tribe. He was instrumental in teaching Native history and culture to children of the community, vital to its preservation. Then, in the 1990s, when the Canadian political landscape began to evolve, he was instrumental in helping to form the structure of the third territory, Nunavut, governed by First Nations.

Years later, the United Church of Canada became the first of the Canadian churches to apologise to Native peoples for wrongdoing during the early part of the twentieth century. Thousands of young Indian boys and girls were pulled from their homes and placed with foster parents to be "civilised." The displacement price was isolation, disillusionment, unemployment and often, alcoholism. The United Church acknowledged their misguided actions in a full apology.

Lorna

As the months sped past with Joyce in her charge, Lorna began to reflect on her own future. She would be sixty in less than two years. It wouldn't be long before she'd need to think about her retirement. With Joyce gone by then, it was a lonely prospect.

Their life together was quiet, but Lorna hoped, fairly content. Joyce passed from the seventh into the eighth grade, and crossed over into her second year in the west. Whatever would she do without Joyce? Lou had been independent all her adult life, and other than the short dalliance with Richard, spent nearly every night of her life alone. But old age was rearing its uncertain head with alarming speed.

There was also a war brewing in Europe, and so soon after the last one! Normally, she was keen for Joyce to be aware of the news, sometimes discussing newspaper articles together over dinner. But in this case, she avoided the subject like the plague. She thought of her nephews in Toronto, inching toward their late teens, and prayed they would not be drafted. That would be a blow like none other for Joyce and Isabelle!

By the time Joyce's second Christmas season in the west arrived, Lorna had made up her mind. One Thursday evening, as she and Joyce sat having dinner, the aging aunt broached the subject which had been on her mind for months.

"You know, Joyce, your time here will soon draw to a close, and you will finally be going home to your mother and brothers. You must be looking forward to that."

"Well, it's still quite a long way off yet, Aunt Lou."

"It will fly by now, I think. Joyce, I've been thinking … I will be retiring soon, and I will miss you terribly when you go back…. I've been thinking I would like to spend my retirement back in Ontario. What do you think about me going with you?"

Taken completely by surprise, Joyce was startled, then delighted. Rushing to her aunt's side of the table, she threw her arms around her neck. "That would be the best thing in the world. That would be wonderful. I would be so happy to have you nearby, Aunt Lou. Now I won't have to worry about missing you when I go back!"

If the truth be told, the idea of returning to Ontario was not just about Lorna's retirement. She had grown so close to her niece, not only was the thought of losing her unbearable, but she also truly hoped she could protect her from further hurt once she returned home.

With Joyce in the picture, Lorna set about writing to her sister to propose the idea. In what seemed like the swiftest response in history, Isabelle replied with enthusiasm, declaring, "That's the best idea I've heard since cars were invented!"

Future Plans

As she sat alone on the bus to and from school, Joyce thought how she had actually been truthful with her aunt. She did prefer to concentrate on her schoolwork. She liked school, or most subjects at least, and if she worked hard and got good marks, she hoped to continue her education when she got older. She really wanted to do something to help other people. With the war breaking out, she thought sadly of soldiers coming home wounded and, in some cases, permanently maimed. She wondered how she might be of some service.

Maybe Andrew was right: the time away from home had given her certain things to think about. When she was busy with her studying, the heavy loneliness which surrounded her most of the time was forgotten.

It seemed useless to hope to make new friends here. She had lost Charlie; she would never see him again. The other girls at school were a closely knit group, had been friends for years and didn't want to let anyone else in. She'd long given up on that idea.

She even wondered if Marg would still be friendly with her when she got back home. Her letter-writing had dropped off, and it was at least six months since she had heard from her. In fact, even Andrew was not as frequent as he used to be in his letter writing. But then, he was working now and had a girlfriend too, according to her mother's last letter. Joyce didn't mind him working, but did he have to have a girlfriend already?

Her mother suddenly seemed to write to her a lot more, telling Joyce all the news of her brothers, a little about her music students and a tidbit or two about her new hobby—weaving.

In addition to the news about Andrew taking a room nearby, Robert had gone off to university on a football scholarship. David had actually skipped a year and was now in high school, and even Billy was going to kindergarten soon!

> *We're all really looking forward to you coming home, Joyce. It won't be long now. And isn't it wonderful that Aunt Lou will be coming back to live with us too! I was thinking ... if she has your old room, you could move upstairs if you like, now the older two have gone. I'm getting everything ready for you.*

Isabelle explained in her letter that both the boarders would be moving out soon, so there would be plenty of room for both Aunt Lou and Joyce. *Just think, Dear, for the first time in years, there will be as many girls as boys!*

Joyce smiled at that idea. It would be quite something ... living with Aunt Lou and her mother! She would soon see Marg again ... if she hadn't made all new friends by now. And oh, to see her brothers again ... especially Andrew and Billy! When she dared to contemplate the thought, she shivered with excitement. She hoped Billy would still remember her.

She wondered how Andrew had accepted having to go to work while Robert was off at university! Especially since Andrew had always been "university material!" With a sigh, she thought how unfair life seemed at times.

Still ... dreams of going home again dominated much of her thoughts ...

Toronto, 1964—A last trip to Grammie's

Alana jumped out of the car and charged toward the big pile of autumn leaves in the corner of the garden. Her brother, Greg, was close on her heels, following by their admonishing parents. "Don't, you'll make a mess of all neat piles!"

She didn't plow into the pile of leaves, she springboarded herself deep into their centre. They were crispy and warm, and held the autumnal smell. Though Alana couldn't articulate that, she shovelled up the oak and maple leaves and breathed in their Septemberness. Their faded pointy edges curled in at her and issued a feeling of Fall comfort, rather than farewell. That grand, Toronto neighbourhood Fall with its towering deciduous trees, and haughty everygreens was just before the move. It was a Fall not of dying off, but of promise. Of new schools, friendships and learning. Above the 10-year-old, shone a mottled canopy of crimson, orange and golden shimmered and dressed up the sunny skies.

Holding up wooden columns which supported its shingled roof, the veranda exuded outdoorsyness yet felt as cosy and warm as the house it cradled. It held familiar scents, of that rambling garden, family memories, and mostly Grammie!

Isabelle appeared at the door —-a small rounded figure composed of four round balls, including her French roller topped with a spikey haircomb sticking out at the top. Her torso, formed from the five children she'd carried and nourished over a 16-year period, was sustained from the sumptuous meals she lovingly cooked, sampled and served her lodgers over a further 35 years. Her bun was like a croissant, or a French roll as she called it, which adorned her like an elegant crown.

'Rayyyy!' (Hurray!) she called to us, as we ran into her arms. 'Rayyyyy, you're finally here.' She didn't bend down, kept upright. But she hugged Alana tight, and Yardley and her cooking scented her welcome. Greg, younger and more reticent joined in. 'C'mon, lunch is ready. They ran through the mosaic-tiled hallway into the grand dining room where the highly carved wooden table was laiden with a smorgasboard—a changing collage of creativity and tradition—the food was always irresistable. They sat in high backed chairs with matching wood carvings, and velvety covers. Pillows sat under Alana and Greg, raising them up for the farewell feast.

Isabelle—Spring 1940

As she practised her pieces for Sunday service, there was a lightness in Isabelle's touch as the piano chords trilled off her fingers. She read the music, practised each hymn a few times, then slid easily off the piano bench to prepare dinner. She floated from one task to another, focused on each one at a time. Exceptionally, she was without worry for tomorrow. The freshness of her relaxed approach was new and unbidden.

But typically, the blissful feeling didn't linger. A sudden flutter of guilt swept over the matriarch, as she thought of how her home would soon be filled with more females than men. She had to admit she had hardly given a thought to missing Robert since he'd left for university. But then, he did come home for Sunday dinners occasionally. It wasn't anything like sending Joyce off to the west! There had been times over the last year and a half when she felt the Lord would punish her for sending her daughter away, and yet here they were…. Joyce was coming home, and not only that, but Lou was too!

Isabelle was very grateful as well that both her elder sons were not going off to war; Andrew, due to his poor vision, and Robert due to his acceptance at university. Although she was very patriotic, she felt her family had already been through enough in recent years and was content that they would be contributing a lot from home.

The return of her daughter and sister along with Andrew's income meant Isabelle could now afford to give notice to her lodgers. Mr. Sharpe was now in a new relationship and planned to remarry, much to Isabelle's relief. She couldn't believe how fortuitous the timing was. It was just Mr. Griffiths she worried about. Where would he go?

Thinking about things a little more, Isabelle worked out all the accommodation. As Robert was off at university, David could have his little cubby hole for a short time. As Andrew was only around the corner, she didn't feel comfortable with anyone taking over his room as yet. Soon, though, he and his new bride would have their own home. Perhaps Mr. Griffiths could stay on a little longer if he wanted to.

But what a lovely thought that all "the girls" could be together downstairs, and the boys upstairs.

Perhaps Joyce and Lorna could share a room for a while. They were used to being together after all.

In the summer of the 1940, the inside of the Canadian National Rail train held very different scenes than two years previously, as Joyce returned to Ontario with her aunt at her side. En route to Edmonton, the trip seemed much, much longer than the two days and two nights it took, whereas the return journey passed in a flash.

Sharing conversations and meals, chatting about their plans after they reached their home province, and meeting a few fellow passengers made for an uneventful but seamless passage. This trip was about homecoming, for both of them.

It has been said that personality is formed by aged three and moral character, the ability to distinguish right from wrong, comes with the maturity of a twelve-year-old. Joyce was now fourteen, and a world away from the twelve-year-old girl who left home two years earlier.

And for Isabelle, by the time the carriage trailed into the Toronto station, she barely recognised her two close family members. Two years and twenty years between sightings of her daughter and sister respectively meant it was like meeting strangers. After exchanging stares for several minutes, they shared a quick triple hug, with three pairs of breasts pressing against each other for the first time.

Then, the mother of five was bursting with news for them. She was sorry the others hadn't managed to come along to meet them, but as they knew, Andrew was working, Robert was away at university, and David, now a teenager, was old enough to stay with Billy.

"The bed situation has been resolved even further," she announced.

Subdued by their puzzlement, the travellers from the West slipped into silence for the journey back to 157 Elliot Street.

Isabelle filled in the blanks for them with an update. Andrew had suddenly announced his engagement to Carol around the corner. He had been invited by Carol's brother to play ping pong there a few times and they had hit it off. Her parents had recently suggested he move into their spare room until he and Carol were married.

"Oh, did you have a pleasant journey?" Isabelle added. "I'm so pleased you're home."

Homecoming

Billy, at nearly six, warmed to his older sister as though there had been little or no hiatus, and that relationship remained close. Equally, the provocations from David continued to cause some disruption to the household, but thankfully with diminished frequency.

Robert, on rare visits home, rushed to embrace his younger sister with playful affection before quickly dashing outside to find someone to toss a football around with.

Andrew, newly engaged, and working full time, had a large part of his time taken up, but when he did come home to dinner, he and a delighted Joyce had long conversations about everything from his new job to her schoolwork and plans for her future. However, Joyce, now fourteen, did not warm to Andrew's fiancée. Carol's entrance into Andrew's life permanently altered the dynamics of her relationship with her eldest brother.

Leaving Home for Adulthood

Those intervening years between Joyce's return to Toronto and her departure for nurse's college about forty miles away in Hamilton were challenging as family dynamics shifted. From being the middle child, before her hiatus in western Canada, Joyce was now the eldest offspring in the household and a good deal of responsibility was shifted onto her shoulders, often sooner than the young teenager was prepared for it.

The large five-bedroom home and its inhabitants lumbered its women with constant demands and Joyce was recruited for a huge portion of the work. Becoming like a second mother to her two younger brothers, she helped them with their homework and refereed the occasional dispute, while helping with the laundry and cooking. At the same time, she tried to keep up with her own increasingly heavy schoolwork. The strain of it all took its toll.

For Lorna, as the elder of the two sisters sharing a home, the move was more of an adjustment than she expected. She was used to her own ways. Isabelle, as the owner of the house and the mother to the children, was equally particular about how things ought to be done. The initial novelty gave way to a certain starchy domestic tolerance and Joyce often found herself torn between trying to please them both.

Joyce remained very fond of her Aunt Lou, with whom she enjoyed a closer relationship than with her mother. Unfortunately, however, this fuelled another level of tension between the two sisters. Lorna, with the benefit of age, endeavoured to defer to Isabelle in every way possible, but the atmosphere at home held a persistent. strain.

Tragically, the perceived rejection, feeling unwanted, never left Joyce. In fact, the alienation, separation from the family, though largely repressed as they were lived, began to build in intensity, and Joyce struggled with depression.

At least her academic dedication paid off well and, unusual for girls of the time, gained her senior matriculation and a place at nursing college. There, she made a few friends, and gained a nursing diploma with honours. Upon graduation, she joined the Victorian Order of Nurses, working in private homes, and then in hospital settings.

She loved nursing, and soon met and married Timothy, a WWII air force veteran who became an insurance executive. The couple became very close to Timothy's sister, Emily, and her husband, Richard, a pilot. In fact, the two women shared the same doctors, and remarkably, were due to give birth on the same day: Joyce to her second child, and Emily to her first.

Tragically, three weeks before their due date, Richard was killed in a plane crash. Their doctor recommended bed rest for Emily, but Joyce insisted that as a Registered Nurse, she could look after her sister-in-law.

With a grieving wife and expectant mother to care for, and heavily pregnant herself, Joyce began to internalise all her worries. Emily delivered a baby boy, Ricky, on time, while Joyce waited three long weeks before her son, Greg, was born. As a single mother, Emily needed to return to work immediately. Joyce took on childcare arrangements for her sister-in-law to allow that to happen. As a mother herself, with a two-year-old to look after, a baby allergic to milk and another infant who struggled to eat, combined with a husband with high standards, her domestic life overwhelmed her. She plunged into depression.[1] Tragically, it was a condition from which she never recovered.

---

[1] Recent research has highlighted genetic predisposition to hypersensitive characters. Common among both men and women in about twenty per cent of the population, the brain activities of those who are easily upset, prone to being deeply hurt by words, or situations, to process the detail of life more thoroughly. They often are burdened with a high intellect.

Guelph, 1964

The new home, the new place, the new town, the new life, in a newly built house, was in a brand-new subdivision. "What's a subdivision?" Alana's brother Greg had asked.

"It's a new section of a city, where they build new houses." Their Dad was excited and very proud. "We're going to have a brand-new house with a fireplace and it's even got knotty cedar panelling. Knotty cedar! Not knotty pine, but knotty cedar! That's not naughty like when you're misbehaving, by the way—it's a type of wood." Their father had giggled for several minutes, enjoying his own joke.

"It's going to be close to my new work and you'll have a new school to go to too." Everything was going to be new that September. "Listen," he continued, "we're going to have a much bigger yard and there's a rec room and another room with a built-in desk for you to do your homework at. You'll have a new bedroom too of course." New friends weren't mentioned. Their dad's excited eyebrows lifted as he told them about the move and what it would mean for them all.

A short time before the move, their father visited to the building project that would become their new home. "They've used black mortar! Black mortar! I specifically asked for grey mortar! Black will look terrible with the white brick. They're ripping it all out and doing it again. It better be ready by moving day." The colour of the mortar was very important.

It was ready. But only just.

When the day came, the family of four followed the moving van into their new driveway, where a large, white-bricked house with white pillars supported a big square porch which lay waiting for them. The house had large front, back and side yards, four bedrooms, three bathrooms and a finished family room. Alana ran inside to investigate. Greeted by the smell of newness, the little girl charged upstairs and found her new room. Her dresser had already been placed there and she opened her shoulder bag to find a family brooch her grandmother had given her, a diary from her aunt, and a photo of her cousin Danny. She stroked the belongings fondly and closed the drawer protectively. She then went down the stairs, bypassing the main floor to the next floor down to find the "rec" room and the den. That was where there was the built-in desk their Dad had talked about, nestled against a wall with built-in bookshelves.

She only ended up doing her homework there a few times. The room with the built-in desk, the built-in library and the built-in beds, they called the den. But to the little girl, it was always Mother's den. Mother seemed to claim it quite quickly, and it became her den, the place where she went for her afternoons. Would the family become "built-in" eventually?

So, it must have been only the first couple of weeks or so after they had moved when the little girl was sitting in the den in front of her homework. A frightening social studies workbook was open in front of her on the built-in desk, and next to it, arithmetic homework threatened. Then, there was grammar and spelling. At least she liked those. Especially spelling. She always saved it for last, like the delicious icing on a cake. But ... social studies and arithmetic ...!

"You've got everything you need to do your homework right there down in the den, Alana. Way you go," her Dad said after supper. Greg didn't seem to have any homework, so while he played in his room, and her parents were sipping their cocktails in the living room, Alana strained her brain to try to find the answers to the questions on the work pages.

Behind the desk, the reddish-brown stripes on the single bedspread rippled into its sagging midriff. The bed had been left hurriedly, without straightening.

When the answers didn't come after quite a long time, her eyes looked up high, high on the shelves. Above her, stood strong rows of hard backed books in dark colours of blue, red and grey—Thackeray, Blackmore, Elliot, Joyce.

Grandmother Isabelle later said when she visited, that they all looked rather "edifying" lining the shelves in the new study. Grammie called it the study instead of the den. Alana didn't ask her what "edifying" was; she thought she should already know. Instead, she just let the feeling the words gave her settle over her and spent a little while gazing at the books every time she went into the room.… And breathing in their old salty smell.

As she struggled to settle to her homework, Alana looked at the rows of serious books for a while. Then she sat looking at pictures … pictures in her mind, of an old life. She thought of her handball game, played all summer against the wall of the old house. "Or-di-nary… moooo-ving." The memory played a familiar song.

She realised she hadn't seen the ball since they'd moved. She'd wanted to place it among her precious things in her dresser drawer. She asked everyone in her family if they had seen it, but no one said they had. The game, called, "Ordinary, moving" had happened in real life. They had moved, but what was the moving about? Like the name of the game—Was it going to be ordinary? Was it going to be "normal"?

Her Mother had a handball which she kept in a little drawer in her bedroom. It had been given to her by her younger brother twenty-five years earlier. However, she'd forgotten it was there, so it was never mentioned or shown to Alana.

Her parents told Alana the small town was friendly, friendlier than the big city they had come from.

When they lived in Toronto, Alana asked her mother once how far away from them her grandmother lived. After a long pause her mother told her it was "about three cigarettes." Then, when pressed by her daughter, she conceded with an edgy laugh. "Oh, about half an hour's drive. There is a train station there, you know, you can take the train from here in Guelph when you're older."

The thirty-minute trip back home was always spent in silence, but once they arrived, Alana chased out of the car and ran up the steps to Grammie's big wraparound veranda, always waiting there, stretching its arms out to welcome her.

Sweeping around two sides of the large house, the shelter held three big wicker chairs with floppy pillows, and plenty of rickety tables with little drawers, where games of jacks and playing cards were secreted away. Loose pairs of slippers were tucked away here and there, and fringed blankets were stacked up in a corner. Topping the tables were jugs and knickknacks, souvenirs from family travels, baskets of tomatoes, apples, beans and chestnuts waiting to be brought inside to be chopped, peeled and cooked. A battered woven shelf stood at the end of the L-shaped porch, holding the preserves from last year. During the fall, on the sprawling lawn, there were heaps of leaves to jump in. Inside the big three-story home, there were large rooms to run around in.

Her favourite was the parlour, with its tall red curtains you could hide behind.

There was even a bay window you could sit beside, look through and have a daydream. Something warm and delicious was always in the oven, sending out irresistible aromas and just waiting to be shared. Alana loved the piano with the metronome you could set to go faster or slower. Covered dishes with coloured candies and mixed nuts nestled on the piano top as well.

But best of all, there was Grammie. She smelled of warm cooking and Yardley's perfume. She taught you songs to play, told you stories, read you books, and served you warm cookies from the oven.

Alana's Mom and Dad thought the neighbourhood was great. There was the doctor and his wife next door with the six kids, including Catherine and Elaine, who, at one year apart were around the same age as the ten-year-old, and they soon included her in many of their family activities. There was also a dentist, a lawyer, a professor or three, a colleague of Alana's father's—life was wonderful in the new subdivision.

Walking to Work

Starting out on the second week of this new walking routine, Alana's Dad, Tim, began to reflect a little en route. "I really thought and hoped this move would be good for us—good for Joyce. To move to a smaller place, where you know your neighbours, maybe get away from the big city. Her brothers have all moved out of Toronto now anyway, and she and her mother ... well ... they've drifted apart. This change will do her some good, I think. Shame she never had a sister. I always said she could have my two," he added, smiling to himself, "and I'd take a couple of her brothers!"

But … he wasn't sure the move was working out in the way that he'd hoped.

With its grey mortar, there were echoes of grey areas around the house. Was it a good move? Alana's mother also often said, "It's wonderful living in a small town!" She had joined a bridge club, did a bit of volunteer work, and … a lot of knitting.

Alana played with the next-door neighbours. One girl older, one girl younger, they sandwiched her age. They didn't skip or play ball, but they would watch tv together. Then, one day in late October, the ten-year-old found herself walking home from school with a friend who lived not too far away and she invited Alana to join her at Girl Guides and the junior church choir. When she attended, she adored every minute. It was only at home that life was lonely. But Greg was the only one whose longing found a strong voice. He missed his cousin terribly. Often, he could be heard pleading, "So, let's move back ta Taraaana!"

Their father ignored these routine rantings. Their mother initially dismissed them, then demurred slightly. Little by little, the perpetual drip feed of pleas to return to Toronto penetrated into their Mom, who surprised them all one day, by saying, "Maybe we *should* go back."

The idea washed over Alana without much residue at the time. As a ten-year-old, she already recognised that they had moved to Guelph because of her dad's job. Therefore, they would stay put because of Dad's job, unless he was transferred again. She had met a few more friends in the neighbourhood while walking to and from school. With her church activities, life was fairly full for a ten-year-old … even if neither of her parents were home very much.

The First Day She Knew...

One November day, Alana arrived home from school to find her mother at the door, all decked out in her best clothes: high heels, a smart suit with a fine brooch and matching hat. "Oh, Alana, I'm off to play bridge," she said, bustling with her daughter as she reached for the car keys. The little girl felt happy. Her Mom seemed happy. Really happy.

When Alana's father arrived home some hours later and interviewed her about her mother and her whereabouts, Alana told him his wife seemed happy too.

"How did she seem before she left?"

"She seemed happy, happy to be going to play bridge."

"Did she seem upset or worried at all?"

"No, not to me." Alana struggled to review her mother's mood before she left, agonised over being able to help find her.

When asked later, the ten-year-old couldn't remember if her Dad cooked some eggs for dinner— she could never really remember him ever cooking anything else but eggs. She couldn't even remember if her brother was there or staying with friends. She couldn't remember much at all—just going to bed eventually, then hearing her dad come upstairs, and when he came in to check in on her, Alana burst into tears.

Crying again, not a good move.

The young girl remembered very little about the following days. Her mother did finally come back home, but she then disappeared for many months, hospitalised again.

Filling in More Blanks

Years later, her grandmother, Isabelle explained to Alana that on the night of her disappearance, her Mom had driven the fifty miles to Toronto and checked into a resplendent hotel under an assumed name. The police had finally traced her there. Her grandmother had laughed in recounting the story, adding, "She's done some funny things over the years."

It was the only time Alana could remember hearing of her mother checking into a hotel. As far as the young girl could remember, her mother only ever checked into the hospital.

If Joyce was going to come home, Alana really wanted her to be all better and never get ill again. But it never worked out that way. She would come home, get ill again, be hospitalised for a few months, come home, get ill, be hospitalised for even longer, maybe even six months.

During many long absences, there were times Alana didn't see her mother for a weekend—or even a couple of hours. It seemed to her that her mother was taken to hospital to get her away from her life and her family but not to make her better.

Gradually, as she got older, Alana often became anxious at the prospect of her mother's return home after a long hospital stay. Would she be better for good this time? Will she finally become like her friends' mothers?

Whenever her mother returned home, her grandmother always prepared a special meal. Accompanying a succulent roast dinner with potatoes, gravy and vegetables, there was tempting cold dishes of jiggly jellies and Waldorf salads, bowls of pickles and olives, garnishing a polished dining table. Several steaming pies awaited for dessert, but Alana found she had no appetite.

Just then, she preferred to play outside. Where was her ball? "Or-di-nary Mooooo-vings," she was already chanting silently in her head while the family tucked in. Alana began to sing as she threw the ball against the new house wall.

"Or-di-nary - that was ordinary. You threw the ball against the wall and you caught it. Moooo-vings. That one was funny because you threw the ball but you didn't move. Just caught it. Then laughing, that was easy. You threw the ball and laughed quickly before catching it. Talking, you just pretended to talk. One hand, you just threw the ball and caught it with one hand. The other hand, you threw and caught with the other hand. One foot, you lifted one foot. And then the o-ther foot, same again. Clap at the front, you clapped, then caught the ball. Clap at the back, You clapped behind your back. Tweedles, you circled your hands around each other. Twidles, the same but the other direction. Curtsy, you did a little curtsy of course. Bowsy, you bowed. Then exercises, you had to clap under and above your leg. Alana always seemed to manage those movements fairly well. But the last one, she had not yet managed to master. For the very last movement of the game, you had to throw the ball and turn around on the spot and catch the ball before it bounced. It was called "Away She Goes" Alana practised and practised that final one but try as she might she never quite managed to master it.

Final Thoughts

Note: There were theories that Joyce suffered some sort of abuse on the train journey, or even during her time in the West. But there has been no evidence of this brought to bear. It was simply the feelings of isolation from the family that played on her mind. Early married life also presented unexpected challenges, as highlighted above. A chemical imbalance in the brain was triggered and sadly Joyce managed to neither enjoy a full life nor life as a well woman.

It's important to emphasize here that research has shown that it is not so much the incident itself which causes a person stress, but how they as an individual respond to it, and critically, their ability to ask for the help they need, and knowing where to find it.

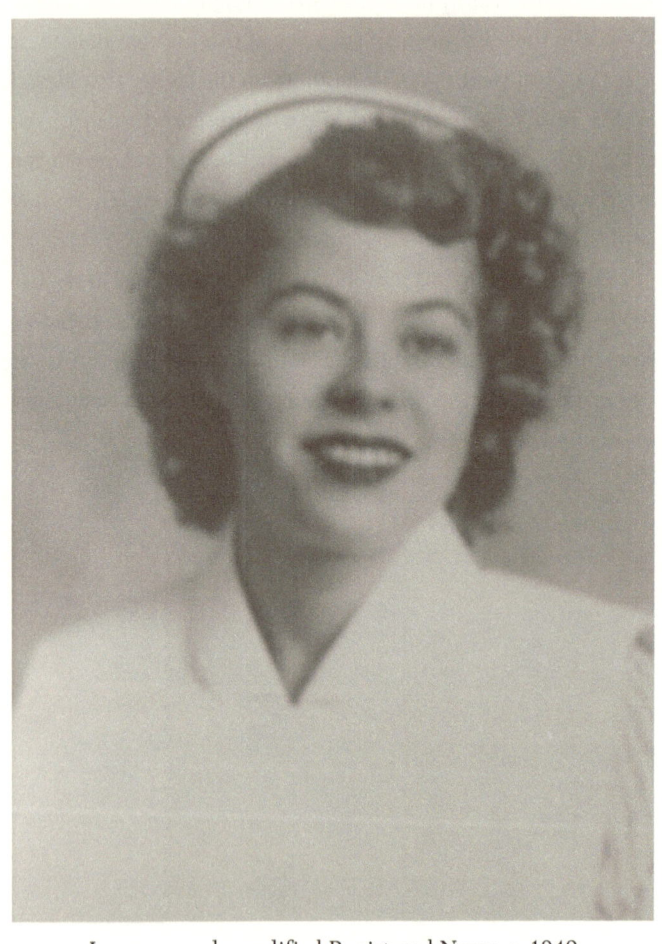

Joyce as newly qualified Registered Nurse c. 1949

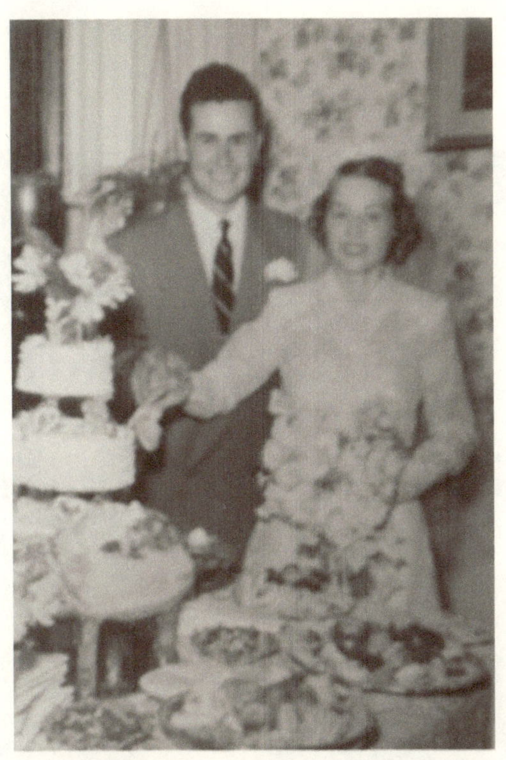

Joyce and Timothy on their wedding day, 1950

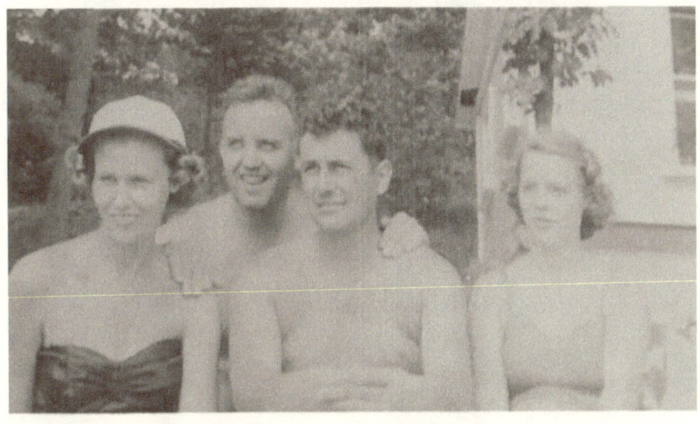

Joyce, husband Timothy, and family c. 1952

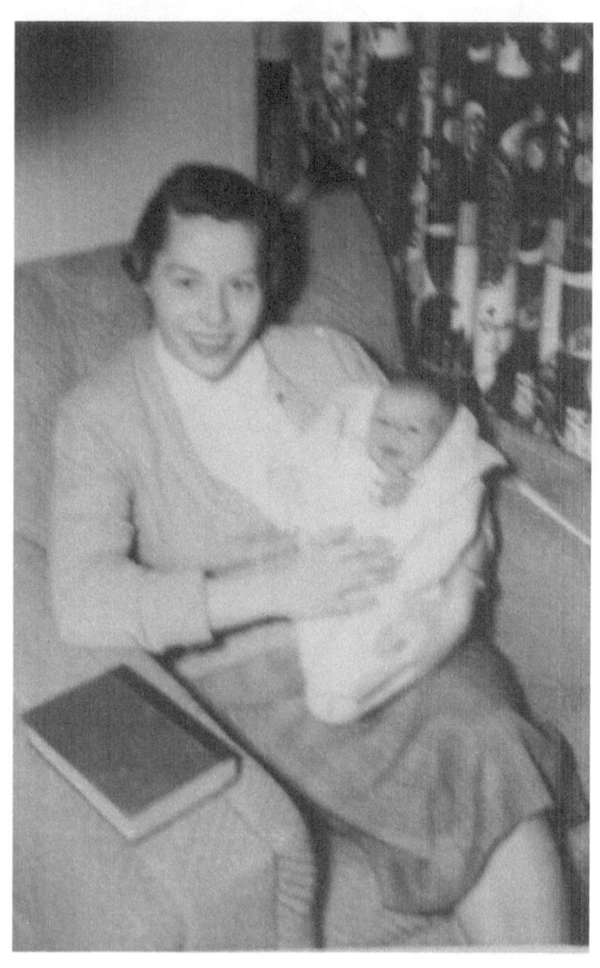

Joyce with baby daughter, Alana, 1954